"From the introduction to th[e] book *Giving Thanks for a Pe[rfectly]* late and learn. Michele has a [...] chair with a cup of coffee and [...] well-crafted words from front to back. This book encourages us to give ourselves and others grace for the imperfect and to press on toward excellence, led by the Lord God. What a great gift for yourself, as well as those you love who need encouragement to keep going!"

—**Robyn Besemann, author of** *Chained No More*

"With this beautifully written book, Michele takes you on a journey with God that you won't want to end. Using everyday challenges and struggles we all face, she highlights how God shows up when you give him your hurts and imperfections. This book will be life altering if you let Michele's wisdom guide you into a deeper relationship with God."

—**Lucille Williams, author of** *From Me to We* **and** *The Intimacy You Crave*

"Overwhelmingly aware of your weaknesses? Join the crowd! We all deal with our slightly imperfect tendencies—we just don't want others to see them. *Giving Thanks for a Perfectly Imperfect Life* helps us be open, honest, and real with God, others, and ourselves. In her witty and loving way, Michele Howe helps us remove the facade of perfection and encourages us to embrace God's perfection. Each chapter is filled with insight, inspiration, and practical applications. You're sure to find strength and peace as you glean the rich truths in this book."

—**Karol Ladd, author of** *The Power of a Positive Woman*

"Through spiritual guidance and gentle self-reflection, author Michele Howe reframes your challenges and disappointments. Equipped with new vision, you can embrace and cherish the winsome beauty of your uniquely imperfectly perfect life."

—**PeggySue Wells, best-selling author of 29 books, including** *The Slave across the Street, Homeless for the Holidays,* **and** *Chasing Sunrise*

"I was hooked on this book from the beginning. Michele describes my obsession with things being perfectly perfect. My perfectly imperfect life has gotten in the way many times of my worship, ministry, and serving others. Michele gives the tools necessary to live a perfectly imperfect life for our Father. From the 'Take-away Action Thought' in each chapter to 'My Heart's Cry to You, O Lord,' you will be filled with ways to be truly thankful for your life."

—Linda Ranson Jacobs
Author, Trainer, Consultant
Developer of DC4K, DivorceCare for Kids
Church Initiative Ministry Ambassador

"If you've ever struggled with not being perfect enough—in your past or your present life—this book is for you! Michele Howe weaves powerful true stories together with profound biblical truth and reminds us that it's time to thank God for our perfectly *imperfect* lives. The biggest take-aways are the concise chapter summaries and action steps that help each of us know what to do next, as we seek to embrace truth and live fruitful lives in the middle of our imperfections. This is an important book!"

—Carol Kent, Speaker and Author
*Staying Power: Building a Stronger
Marriage When Life Sends Its Worst*

"One of my great disillusionments is that the older I get the more imperfect life seems to feel. I so appreciate how Michele Howe gives us hope, help, and heavenly freedom from the unrealistic picture-perfect pursuit of trying to have everything 'just right.' *Giving Thanks for a Perfectly Imperfect Life* will help you exhale, smile, and even embrace your beautifully imperfect life."

—Pam Farrel, author of over 50 books, including
the best-seller *Men Are Like Waffles, Women Are Like Spaghetti*

Giving Thanks for a Perfectly IMPERFECT Life

MICHELE HOWE

Giving Thanks for a Perfectly IMPERFECT Life

HENDRICKSON
PUBLISHERS

an imprint of Hendrickson Publishing Group

Giving Thanks for a Perfectly Imperfect Life

© 2020 Michele Howe

Published by Hendrickson Publishers
an imprint of Hendrickson Publishing Group
Hendrickson Publishers, LLC
P. O. Box 3473
Peabody, Massachusetts 01961-3473
www.hendricksonpublishinggroup.com

ISBN 978-1-68307-293-5

All rights reserved. No part of this book may be reproduced or transmitted in any form or by any means, electronic or mechanical, including photocopying, recording, or by any information storage and retrieval system, without permission in writing from the publisher.

Scripture quotations contained herein are taken from the Holy Bible, New International Version®, NIV®. Copyright © 1973, 1978, 1984, 2011 by Biblica, Inc.™ Used by permission of Zondervan. All rights reserved worldwide. www.zondervan.com. The "NIV" and "New International Version" are trademarks registered in the United States Patent and Trademark Office by Biblica, Inc.™

Printed in the United States of America

First Printing — June 2020

Library of Congress Control Number: 2020934798

To my husband, Jim,
and our children Nicole, Katlyn, Corinne, and James

Thank you for never making me feel guilty for spending
so much time huddled in my little basement office. I know
there were moments when I was distracted by looming
deadlines and focused solely on finishing just one more page
when I called out "I'll be up in a minute!" but I wasn't.

Never once did any of you complain that dinner
was a little late or that you had to wait longer than
you wanted to ask me an important question.

For all the love and patience and support
you extended to me over these years,
I want to tell the world that I am so grateful for our family.
I love you all so much!

 Contents

Acknowledgments

S ometimes words lack the power punch I want them to land as I seek to express my gratitude to everyone at Hendrickson Publishers who labored over this book that you, dear reader, are now holding in your hands. It all starts with a book's conception in the mind of an author (me), which leads to receiving the delightfully heartening news that my favorite publisher (Hendrickson!) once again agreed to publish my latest book idea. After that follow countless hours spent writing, editing, designing the cover (and writing back cover copy) and the interior pages, all finally resulting in the actual physical production of this book.

Amazing, isn't it? The sheer number of individuals—who lend their expertise to a project like this so that readers like you can be uplifted, encouraged, and gently challenged to grow in your knowledge of Jesus Christ as his beloved disciple—is staggering to me. I've been in publishing for over thirty-five years, and I'm still wowed by the intricate and demanding process of creating a book.

Let me now name some names so that you, dear reader, can join me in saying thank you to these marvelously talented and God-honoring individuals whom I am so thankful to call my friends from afar. First, thank you, Patricia Anders; as editorial director at Hendrickson, you carry many responsibilities, and I cannot imagine the heavy workload you carry every day—

seemingly with perfect ease. I am so thankful for you and for the friendship we now enjoy, and I'm so excited we can say together, "We did it. Again! Let's celebrate!" To Meg Rusick for marketing, Phil Frank for typesetting, and Sarah Slattery for cover design, my most sincere appreciation and thanks for working so hard on behalf of my book. Every single time, you give me a priceless gift by laboring each in your own specific area of expertise to build these precious books with me. Thank you. Thank you. Thank you! Finally, to Dave Pietrantonio, who handles the book production process, kudos once again for making all the pieces come together in such an eye-appealing and practical way. You are much appreciated.

I also want to express my kindest appreciation to Bob Hostetler, who happily represents me at the Steve Laube Agency. Keep the jokes coming, Bob. We writers tend to be all too serious, and your sense of humor brings me daily comedic relief when I need it most.

 Introduction

"If the Son sets you free, you will be free indeed."
John 8:36

I am a perfectionist. I admit it. I was, at one time long ago, pretty proud of the fact.

Looking back, I cannot for the life of me understand why I would have considered my perfectionist tendencies as anything positive and God-honoring. But I did. Just to prove to you that I know of what I speak, I will share with you a few of my earlier perfectionist, soul-crushing habits.

As a child, I recall being obsessed with symmetry. Pictures, books, rugs, knick-knacks, anything and everything had to square up in a perfectly balanced way or I'd succumb to this irrepressible urge to "fix it." I recall lying on my bed and looking around my bedroom, and if the tiniest edge of the curtain was even a bit crooked, I would quickly get up and straighten it.

Every night when I went to bed, I would make sure my blankets and sheets were pressed smoothly from every angle and tucked in just so. Then I would carefully slip in between the sheets and, you guessed it, straighten them again before closing my eyes. Oh, and my clothes had to be a perfect match in color too. Had. To. Match. I recall driving my poor mother to distraction with that particular perfectionist must-do. If you looked in my closet, you would have been impressed. It was perfect. From top to bottom, my clothes, shoes, and toys were

1

positioned in proper order according to my perfectionist obsession for symmetry.

Now that you have the picture of how I dealt with my surroundings and possessions on the outside, I'll let you into the inner workings of my child's heart and mind. My inside was the mirror opposite of my perfect external world. Because of my fear-driven perfectionist tendencies, I strived for control in every area. I felt mostly anxious, afraid, and high-strung because—let's face it—children do not have much control of anything, large or small, in their little worlds. I remember developing what I called "my exit strategy" for any situation I was uncomfortable with. I would imagine the worst that could happen (at school, at home, at my dance classes) and then create my exit strategy (or my coping plan), just in case the worst actually did transpire. I was contemplating these exit strategies as an *early elementary-aged child*. How sad is that?

Anyone who admires and desires to emulate the perfectionists among us has no idea the mental and emotional torture we perfectionists put ourselves through on a daily basis. How eternally thankful I am that God sent one of his ambassadors to me when I was twelve years old to share the good news of the gospel, whereupon I immediately repented and accepted Jesus' perfect sacrifice on the cross for my sins. God knew my anxious child's heart was in dire need of saving, rescue, and eternal security. On that momentous and life-changing holiday evening just before Christmas, my new life began and God started the process of setting me free from the self-imposed perfectionist prison I had created for myself.

It's been a lifelong process—this being set free from old soul-crushing habits and sinful control issues—but I can truthfully say that today, all these years later, I'm becoming freer by the day. I thank God for helping me take step after step away from relying on my exit strategies and my Plan Bs. These days,

I know my Savior personally and profoundly, and he knows me. I know God is the only one I can turn to when I am in need of rescue, and he is the only one who can truly secure my rescue. My eternal security is a heavenly destination. Knowing—*really* knowing—these truths helps me stay in step with the Spirit when I am tempted to massage, manipulate, and manage my life according to my former perfectionist patterns.

My hope and prayer is that as you read about fellow sojourners (like me) who struggle with perfectionist habits and tendencies, you will be looking for God's presence, grace, strength, and transforming power in each and every circumstance. For us perfectionists, accepting our weaknesses, flaws, and failures is a difficult pill to swallow. But swallow our pride we must if we are to reap the blessed freedom found only in letting go of our binding perfectionist mind-sets.

"If the Son sets you free, you will be free indeed," Jesus tells us. What perfectionist doesn't want to experience freedom from anxiety, failure, control, rejection, peer pressure, fear of not being good enough, and a host of other dreaded imperfect or imagined outcomes? As we grow in the grace and knowledge of God, we can experience this supernatural freedom from the inside out. This journey to inner freedom begins when we make Jesus our Lord and Savior, but let's not forget the vital element of developing a consistently grateful heart on our journey to inner freedom. As we learn to give thanks for our perfectly imperfect lives, we set in motion a supernatural principle that sets us free from the inside out in ways we could have never imagined. Are you ready to see what God can do with a perfectionist who wants to live a free and faith-fueled life? Then let's get reading!

 Chapter 1

Perfectly Imperfect—You and Me

And the God of all grace,
who called you to his eternal glory in Christ,
after you have suffered a little while, will himself restore you
and make you strong, firm and steadfast.
1 Peter 5:10

The secret is Christ in me, not me in a
different set of circumstances.
Elisabeth Elliot

I was well into the second hour of trying to untangle a skein of yarn and my fingers were aching, no longer exhibiting the nimble dexterity they had when I first started. This all too frequent and simultaneously irritating aspect of knitting happens almost every time I begin a new project. I love yarn—the textures, the colors, and the possibilities of what can be created. I hate the untangling of it. Love/hate. I can almost feel my blood pressure rise when I reflect back over the time I spent trying to unravel a simple knot out of a skein of yarn before I could start knitting once more. All I want to do is knit, I think to myself. Is it really that complicated?

Sitting there with a tangled mess of yarn spilling over my legs and onto the rug at my feet, I finally shook my head in despair and reached for the scissors. Enough, I told myself. I have wasted enough time trying to save a few feet of yarn. I've endured enough aggravation for being foolish enough to repeat a mistake I've made so many times before (my mom taught me to always take the time to create a ball of yarn from its original skein so it won't tangle). I've expended enough emotional energy, which was zapped all because I wanted to fix something that went awry. Enough. Enough. *Enough.*

Impatiently, I cut the threads of yarn layered in knots and tangles, and I experienced something akin to sad resignation. I felt like I had just lost a fight. A battle with a skein of yarn no less! But then I realized a valuable lesson from this, and I thought to myself how often I got tied up in internal knots whenever something (little or large) went wrong. On that particular afternoon when I sat trying to untangle my yarn in vain, I realized I was also trying to work through a conversation I had with my husband in vain. Let's just say this: all the irritation, impatient aggravation, and emotional energy zapping was not solely on account of my battle with the knots in the yarn. It was much more personal and much more painful.

As I considered my husband's words to me the previous afternoon, I knew one thing for sure: They were spoken in love. He wants the very best for me, and he isn't afraid of speaking hard truths when I need it. And I needed it. After a fast-paced, activity-filled summer with lots of happy interaction with our adult children, their spouses, and our grandchildren, I was nursing a private hurt from a couple of conversations that, from my perspective, went south fast. I was preoccupied with my own emotional heart pain, and I kept bringing it up to my husband. When I say preoccupied, I am speaking of the over-the-top preoccupation that perfectionists indulge in, and then make excuses when they get all fired up about something that didn't work out as they had expected, planned, or predicted. My thoughts revisited and then sinfully lingered on these conversations so much that I was losing my joy, my peace, and my purpose. I felt stuck in an imperfect mess of my own making.

Cue in the biblical words of challenge and gentle rebuke from my loving spouse. But I hate it when I'm reminded I can't hide or get away with even a silent stinky attitude that dishonors God, because my spouse knows me too well. There I was trying to untangle both that dratted yarn and my emotions, and it wasn't pretty. After I not so gently cut the threads of yarn that caused me so much inner angst, I began to cut through the issues of my troubled heart that were getting me all tangled and knotted up as well. I started to realize that, once again, my fixation on getting things right (code for "perfect") hindered me from what God really wanted me to see and understand. This revelation was the starting point for me to cry out to God and ask him to help me recast the events that were stinging in my heart and memory and see them through his big-picture, eternal (and divinely perfect) lens.

God began to show me that I had been nursing an overly confident attitude as a Christian wife and mom who believed she could skillfully traverse even the most difficult conversations with her adult children, their spouses, and her grandchildren without ever erring by what she said (or did not say). I was banking on my own abilities (my experience, maturity, and selfless heart motives toward my family) to achieve the impossible. There's a word for that: pride. When I quieted myself before the Lord long enough to hear him break through my wounded and resistant heart, I understood, once again, that God never expects me to be perfect but he does expect me to grow in grace and maturity day by day. He knows perfection isn't possible this side of heaven.

What God wants of me is to accept this painful reality, this perfectly imperfect me, and thank him for his amazing grace and supernatural ability to bring good out of my goof-ups.

Sting though it may, any delusion we perfectionists cling to that we can get "it" right all the time is a lie from the pit of hell. So God, in his great mercy, allows me (and you) to suffer (by accepting the truth of our human failings and accompanying sinfulness) so that we can be restored in strength and steadfastness. God knows that these character qualities will see us through the challenges of life far better than trusting in our delusions of self-perfection. Thank the good Lord with me for the faithful folks in our lives who love us enough to tell us the truth about ourselves we don't want to see. Perfect? Never. A divine work in progress? Yes—thankfully!

Every one of us is preoccupied with something or someone. If your preoccupation doesn't fall under the something or someone categories, perhaps it is the attainment of some dream, hope, or desire. I love the quote above by Elisabeth Elliot when she says that the secret is Christ in her, not her in a different set of circumstances. I have to remind myself of that every day. Today, this very minute, am I choosing to preoccupy myself with my myriad flaws and weaknesses? Or will I choose to set my heart, mind, and soul on God and knowing him better? I believe that much of my inner heart's angst comes from a lack of contentment in how God made me with my specific personality, giftedness, preferences, and passions. I struggle against believing the lie that if I were "all together" 100 percent of the time, then my illusion of perfection would lessen (or eliminate) my suffering, my struggles, and my pain. But it isn't so.

God help us all to stop our unholy preoccupation with ourselves—our failings, mistakes, and weaknesses, all of which can depress, derail, and keep us from moving forward today in service to God and others. As a recovering perfectionist, I know firsthand that when I am forced to face my failings (cue in the loving spouse!), I rankle against the rebuke. I'd much rather go to my quiet corner and ask for God's forgiveness and then resolve to do better. While this asking for forgiveness is the right biblical response after I have sinned, I believe God wants to take that holy transaction a step farther in my heart and mind. God wants me to fully comprehend that when I am weak (and I am), then this is exactly when God's grace falls on me in strength. Like Paul, I need to look at myself accurately (because God does), and increase my gratefulness quotient for his unconditional love for me that is not dependent on my success or failure. It's only when we truly understand our weakness, our frailty, and our imperfections, and we recognize God's strength, power, and perfection, that our hearts can finally find a place of rest in his love. Let's not get weighed down by our imperfections and preoccupied by our failings.

Rather, let these glaring imperfect human qualities produce in us the humility and dependence on our Lord that he wants for all his beloved children.

 Take-away Action Thought

When I am made painfully aware of my failings and my sinful tendencies, I will confess my sins and immediately begin praising God for his forgiveness and his mercy on me. I will gladly rest in his unconditional love.

My Heart's Cry to You, O Lord

Father, I need to ask your forgiveness for being preoccupied with my weaknesses and my imperfections. I am discovering that the more I focus on what I believe is wrong in me and with me, the less I focus on you. Lord, I need to accept that I will never measure up to a standard of perfection and that you do not expect this of me. I have created a prison of my own making by demanding of myself what I am incapable of achieving. Clothe me, Lord, with a spirit of humility, gratefulness, and contentment. Help me to lean all the harder into your faithful, abundantly merciful arms. Amen.

Giving Thanks for My Perfectly Imperfect Life

1. I will write down specific areas of weakness that trouble me. I will prayerfully ask the Lord to help me see these weaknesses through his perspective, and I will make note of how God has used them to push me closer to him.

2. When I begin to get bogged down by my own imperfections, I will refocus my attention on God rather than on myself. I will search out the Scriptures that describe the character of God and meditate on them.

3. I will purpose to be preoccupied with heavenly things by studying one Old Testament biblical character and reading how God used that person in spite of his/her weaknesses and flaws.

 Chapter 2

Perfectly Imperfect—Our Past

See, I am doing a new thing!
  Now it springs up; do you not perceive it?
I am making a way in the wilderness
  and streams in the wasteland.

Isaiah 43:19

*Our present enjoyment of God's grace tends to be lessened
by the memory of yesterday's sins and blunders. But God
is the God of our yesterdays, and He allows the memory
of them to turn the past into a ministry of spiritual
growth for our future. God reminds us of the past to
protect us from a very shallow security in the present.*

Oswald Chambers

Allie woke up from a restless sleep, wondering for the umpteenth time if she had made the right decision to break up with her boyfriend, Brad, of almost two years. She had prayed about ending the relationship for weeks, but she now had to remind herself why she had ended it. Allie's past record of broken relationships had nothing to do with her being unrealistically picky. She wasn't looking for perfection in a man. Rather, Allie—from her own history of making poor relational decisions—had much understanding and compassion for others with pasts like her own.

What grieved Allie the most after she ended this relationship was that she and Brad had started out as friends. They used to hang out together after church and at various social events with mutual friends, and they even worked out together at the same gym. Seemingly, Allie and Brad had lots in common: faith, friends, activities, interests. While they were happy as friends, Brad had begun to push for more from Allie. He wanted to date his best friend, and eventually he wore down her resistance until she finally agreed.

At first, little changed between them. Both continued to attend the same church, hang out with mutual friends, and see each other at the gym several nights a week. Then, little by little, Allie noticed that whenever she would begin talking about what God was doing her in life, Brad would go strangely quiet. He also no longer had a response to her excitement about serving the local community through their church—and when Allie invited Brad to join her in service opportunities, he refused. No explanation. Just a firm no thanks.

Allie couldn't understand why he was growing more and more resistant to anything related to their faith journey. More distressing, though, was when Brad began pressing Allie to skip Sunday services and forgo their church friend group outings in favor of sports-related activities or short day trips out of the city. Allie's conscience began to stir, quietly at first, but then it felt like a gong would go off whenever Brad tempted her to walk farther and farther away from faith, family, and friends. Allie knew from painful experience with previous boyfriends how quickly one romantic partner can sway and then influence the other—and not always for the good.

It wasn't just that Allie and Brad were heading in different life directions that troubled her. This current relational stress felt all too reminiscent of past failed relationships. One evening after working out with Brad (and after yet another argument about making plans for the weekend), Allie called her mom when she got home. She needed someone who had known her forever and had walked with her through all of her ups and downs of dating to offer some wisdom and advice. Allie shared with her mom every concern she had about Brad before admitting that she wondered if her past mistakes had flawed her permanently. "Nonsense," Mom replied. "Allie, today you are a far different person than you were five years ago. You learned the hard way about making wise choices in dating. But you did learn. Everything about this relationship with Brad had the promise of a great future. There was no way you could have foreseen this change in Brad. This isn't your fault. It isn't anyone's fault. Remember that."

Allie and her mom talked long into the evening. When Allie finally said goodbye, she was comforted and reassured that she had made the best decision in breaking up with Brad. Painful? Yes. Permanently scarring? Definitely not. Allie took her mom's advice and sat down with her journal and began searching out Scripture verses that would strengthen her resolve to trust God and never settle for less than God's best in any relationship. Allie wrote down God's promises and quietly meditated on them late into the night. That evening, when she finally said her goodnights to the Lord, Allie slept better than she had in months.

The past is a powerful entity. By it, we can wisely reflect and glean important lessons from our failures as well as our successes. But our past can similarly paralyze us from making needed decisions today. It can confound us by hindering our willingness to walk boldly into the future with God. The past with all of its pain and hurt and embarrassment can turn us into self-protecting, self-interested, selfish individuals who have ceased trying to live faith-filled lives. As I considered all the relational pain that Allie had endured from past unhealthy relationships, I felt for her. I could imagine myself in her position and understand why Allie may have been second-guessing her ability to discern people's characters.

However, that's just one side of the story. True, Allie blundered her way through many unhealthy and ungodly relationships in her early twenties. But then God entered her life, heart, and mind, and he changed everything—from the inside out. God truly did in her what this verse from Isaiah 43:19 promises,

> See, I am doing a new thing!
> Now it springs up; do you not perceive it?
> I am making a way in the wilderness
> and streams in the wasteland.

To hear Allie describe her early dating experiences, she was living in a relational wasteland. But God rescued her and made a way for her to escape the wilderness; he created refreshing streams in which Allie could heal and grow strong again.

The problem with troublesome pasts is that each time we experience a similarly painful encounter in the present, our minds go straight back to those bad times and we begin to wonder. We wonder if we are going to have to endure the same suffering we went through before. We wonder where we went wrong this time around. We wonder if we truly ever learned

14

anything from our past mistakes. We wonder if we're broken people. We wonder where God is in the midst of today's agony.

Admittedly, Allie allowed those painful past memories too much space in her heart and mind after she broke it off with Brad. She had, however, learned much since her early dating days. As a disciple of Christ, she now recognized the powerful strength that comes through a fellow believer's insightful words and encouragement, especially when we are feeling sensitive and emotional about our past mistakes. When Allie articulated her concerns to her mother, those issues moved out into the light of day. Allie and her mom were able to talk through her fears; and in the end, she was stronger, more settled in her faith, and more convinced than ever that God had directed her to end the relationship. Allie did what we all need to do: Stop allowing our pain-ridden pasts to paralyze us in the present. Each of us needs to face our past, imperfect though it is, and press into the truth that God is in the business of creating refreshing streams of life where there was once only wasteland and suffering.

 ## Take-away Action Thought

When I start to allow pain from my past to take hold of my heart and mind, I will stop myself from lingering there. Instead, I will search for God's promises that speak of each day as a new beginning, and I will thank the Lord for walking close beside me into my new season of life.

My Heart's Cry to You, O Lord

Father, I was overwhelmed with emotional pain today, and I had to make a choice that was difficult for me. Even though I'm sure I obeyed you in making this decision, I am sometimes overcome by memories from the past. I start to second-guess my abilities to make wise relational choices. Help me to find my strength and peace in your word. Lead me to those promises that remind me that you are always close by my side and that you will help me day by day. Father, I want to forget all of my past mistakes, but I know that I can also learn from them. Give me the wisdom I need to glean from my poor choices in the past, so that today I can be confident to decide what is best for me and honoring to you. Amen.

Giving Thanks for My Perfectly Imperfect Life

1. Today, I will sit down and make a list of the most painful mistakes I have made. Next, I will search out the Scripture verses that nullify these poor choices through the power of God's redemption.

2. I will memorize this verse from Isaiah 43:19 and say it out loud whenever I start to overthink my past and begin to feel defeated by it: "See, I am doing a new thing! Now it springs up; do you not perceive it? I am making a way in the wilderness and streams in the wasteland."

3. I will write down any decisions I am aware of that I will need to make in the coming weeks, and I will prayerfully ask God to give me wisdom and his divine understanding in each situation. If I am not certain of the way I should take, I will seek out a wise fellow believer and ask for counsel and prayer.

 # Chapter 3

Perfectly Imperfect—Our Present

If you declare with your mouth, "Jesus is Lord," and
believe in your heart that God raised him from the
dead, you will be saved. For it is with your heart
that you believe and are justified, and it is with your
mouth that you profess your faith and are saved.

Romans 10:9–10

*It takes gentleness to be part of what God is doing in someone's
life and not get in the way. It takes patience to deal with the
sin and weakness of those around you. It takes perseverance to
be part of the change in a relationship because that change is
most often a process and rarely an event. It takes forgiveness to
move beyond the times you have been mistreated by another. It
takes forbearance to continue to love a person even when you
are being provoked. It is hard to respond in kindness when
you are treated unkindly. It takes remarkable love to serve the
good of the other person and not be distracted by daily needs.*

Tim Lane and Paul Tripp

I *hate social media!* Julie screamed silently. *I see way too much of what is going on in Gemma's life. I don't want to know how she spends her time on the weekends, partying from Friday evening to Sunday night, wasting her time and money on worthless things. Ugh. I wish I didn't have to tune in to her daily posts just to keep up with what she is doing. But with Gemma living in another country, social media is the best way for me to keep current. I just wish it didn't hurt so much.* Julie stopped reading Gemma's posts and turned to her well-worn Bible and journal. "I know I cannot change my daughter's heart, but I can pray that God will do the impossible," Julie said, as if speaking those sentiments out loud would cement them into reality.

Julie then began reading through her rotation of five psalms followed by a proverb before digging into one chapter in the Old Testament and three chapters in the New Testament. By the time she completed her daily reading, she opened her journal, feeling fortified to enter into warfare prayer for Gemma. Closing her eyes, Julie began praying in earnest for her daughter—her only daughter.

Gemma had been a late-in-life baby for Julie and her husband, Sam. Both Julie and Sam had been schoolteachers, so their work schedule meshed perfectly as they reared their four children. When Gemma came along, they had only ten years of employment left before they could retire. Together, they poured the bulk of their energy and efforts into raising Gemma after their three older boys were off to college. Those were such happy days, Julie recalled fondly, and Gemma was an easy child to parent.

Gemma had been persistent in asking them to take her to church and to youth group. She even led summer camps for kids. Gemma raised her own money to go on overseas missions trips, because she wanted to tell people about Jesus. It seemed they had a pretty perfect parenting experience with Gemma. So what had happened?

Julie had no idea what had changed in Gemma's heart and mind about living for Jesus. *Maybe I'll never know,* Julie thought resignedly. She then wrote down several Bible verses from the day's reading that had struck a chord. The first one was from Romans 10:9–10.

> If you declare with your mouth, "Jesus is Lord," and believe in your heart that God raised him from the dead, you will be saved. For it is with your heart that you believe and are justified, and it is with your mouth that you profess your faith and are saved.

Pausing to reread this powerful truth, Julie suddenly felt a nudge to reopen her computer and check to see if Gemma had posted again. She had. Tears came to Julie's eyes as she read it. "I know I don't talk about my faith very often here, but I want everyone to know that I may not know much, but I do know that Jesus is my savior, my everything: #jesusislord!" *Oh, Lord,* Julie prayed, *thank you! Thank you for this encouragement. It strengthens my heart and my resolve to keep praying. I know things aren't perfect, but this is a wonderful starting place. And the timing is pretty perfect too.*

Today. This day. This present moment. How perfect is it? Depending on our perspective and our commitment to honoring the Lord by refusing to give way to anxiety and other debilitating fears, any (and every) day can be a beautiful day. Given the reality that no day is perfectly perfect, because perfection in its literal sense cannot exist this side of heaven, we are daily challenged to seek for the beauty amid the imperfect that grabs for our attention. Julie's experience (and frustration) with reading her daughter's social media posts had her feeling upset and anxious. She truly despaired for her daughter whenever she read the words that seemed to reveal Gemma's heart online. Wisely, Julie turned away from what was causing her to lose her inner peace.

More important, Julie turned to God and his life-giving word to renew her mind, encourage her heart, and direct her prayers. She took to heart the verses that the Holy Spirit prompted her to add to her journal for further meditation. Once she had quieted her heart, mind, and emotions through Bible study, she closed her eyes to shut out any distractions, and she listened for God's inner voice to speak truth to her hurting mother's heart. Julie did battle for her daughter's heart before the throne of God, all the while assured that Jesus was right there interceding for Gemma's heart as well. Many may say that Julie's decision to find her strength and her words to pray from Scripture were perfect—and I would agree.

Today. This day. This present moment. How perfect is it? For each of us, the answer to that question is found wherever we choose to place our focus. Do we choose to focus on sad and sometimes terrifying real-life situations? On the all too temporary material world that at best serves only to distract us from what matters most? On the challenging interpersonal trials we face with those God has placed in our lives? Whether we forfeit today's peace and contentment for troubles related to a person, place, or thing, it matters little. What makes all the difference in the world (our inner world) is that we choose to take ten good long looks at God for every one short look at our imperfect day (and everyone and everything in it).

Let us not forget that as we pray, God will intercede in the lives of those we love, and that God is also doing a good work within us as we slowly develop the character qualities listed in the quote above. As Lane and Tripp remind us, "It takes perseverance to be part of the change in a relationship because that change is most often a process and rarely an event." Let's purpose in our hearts to follow Julie's example by running straight to God's life-giving word, and then settle ourselves into battle through prayer for what matters most in this life: people's hearts and souls.

 ## Take-away Action Thought

My present attitude about today is in my hands alone. I refuse to be ruled by the trials I see happening around me and to those I care most about. I will run to God's word and make his eternal promises my permanent (and perfect) hiding place.

My Heart's Cry to You, O Lord

Father, please help me to be wise enough to run straight to your word for wisdom, for understanding, and for the encouragement I so desperately need. I often discover that my emotions can easily rule my day if I allow them to supersede your eternal truth. Help me to find my peace and my daily perspective on the troubles in the world at large (and in my small corner of the world) in your promises. Though I long for a perfect day, I realize there is no perfection on this side of heaven. Instead, I must find my hope and help in you and pray through whatever trials and struggles I am facing. Amen.

Giving Thanks for My Perfectly Imperfect Life

1. I will begin and end this day with a heart brimming with gratitude. I will start by listing and then speaking out loud (for everyone to hear) all that I am thankful for. I will refuse to grumble!

2. Today, I will turn the tables on any trials, troubles, or imperfections that burden me by asking God to show me how he can transform each scenario into something beautiful from an eternal perspective.

3. My prayers will be full of praises alone today. I will give thanks for God's listening ear, for Jesus' intercession, and for the Holy Spirit's promptings on who and what to pray for this day. I will sing and offer my praises for who my heavenly Father is, and how thankful I am that I serve a powerful and sovereign God.

 # Chapter 4

Perfectly Imperfect—Our Future

For the LORD God is a sun and shield;
the LORD bestows favor and honor;
no good thing does he withhold
from those whose walk is blameless.
Psalm 84:11

*God has promised to meet all our needs. What
we don't have now, we don't need now.*
Elisabeth Elliot

The recent death of a long distance friend who had suffered from breast cancer, followed by lung cancer that eventually spread to the brain, has made me contemplate life in a deeper way. My friend and I enjoyed a close relationship, all because of one simple act of kindness. She had reached out to me a decade ago, offering to help me gain my author bearings on social media. If you know me, you know that the term "social media" gives me shivers all the way up and down my introverted spine. This friend was a super-extrovert, who in a very winsome and delightfully persuasive manner convinced me that I had to get on board with the social media bandwagon or my writing days were numbered. She was correct.

My dear friend helped guide me to websites and talked me through many a technical glitch as I set up my web page and learned to navigate FB, Twitter, Instagram, LinkedIn, and Pinterest. My faithful friend continued to text, e-mail, or call me with helpful suggestions every few weeks or so. She even had me on her radio program whenever I had new title released. She was, in a word (or two), perfectly wonderful. So fast-forward some eight years later when I receive a call and my friend tells me she has breast cancer and is scheduled to undergo a double mastectomy and then breast reconstruction. After we chatted for a long while, we prayed together. Ending that call, I prayed again, perhaps more because I needed the Lord to calm me down inside. My friend's initial surgery was successful, but it started a progression of complicated cancer-related surgeries and treatments. Months later when we spoke a final time, she asked me to pray for her impending lung surgery. Not long after that conversation, God called her home and her suffering was mercifully over. I simultaneously wept and rejoiced when I heard the news.

My friend's unexpected diagnosis and fast-spreading cancer was a shock to her, her family and friends, and to me. Some days, I still have a sudden urge to text or e-mail her about something going on in my writing world. Then I remember. My friend isn't within texting, e-mailing, or calling range. But I believe she is somewhere far better. It's me and her family and friends who continue to find ourselves reeling in grief mode when we least expect it. But that's what happens in this perfectly imperfect world, isn't it? Illness. Death. Disaster. Financial loss. Job stress. Family struggles. Losses of one kind or another can add up, and then we find ourselves struggling to trust God for our tomorrows. It's so easy to get sidetracked and distracted by what is happening in our "now" that we forget how wonderful our future is guaranteed to be.

My friend wasn't afraid of what was going to happen next. She knew without any doubt that God was in all her tomorrows— be they painful ones here on earth fighting cancer or glorious ones near her Savior in heaven. She wasn't afraid of fighting with all she had in order to live, but neither was she afraid to die. My friend knew this:

> For to me, to live is Christ and to die is gain. If I am to go on living in the body, this will mean fruitful labor for me. Yet I am torn between the two: I desire to depart and be with Christ, which is better by far. (Philippians 1:21–23)

My friend's confidence in the trustworthiness of God is the legacy she left behind to all who knew and loved her.

One of most admirable qualities my friend exhibited during her battle with cancer was that she was wise enough not to look too far ahead into an unknown future. Truly, she lived out what Elisabeth Elliot wrote above:

> God has promised to meet all our needs. What we don't have now, we don't need now.

Read that again.

> God has promised to meet all our needs. What we don't have now, we don't need now.

What, we may ask, do we not need right now? Worry? Fear of our unknown tomorrows? Anything and everything we can't control—which is everything! You name it, and we as frail humans have fretted over it.

While I can attest to the priceless value of all the social media mentoring my friend provided over the years, what she taught me most were the life lessons on facing the future with a fearless confidence in the absolute faithfulness of God to supply our every need. She didn't know what her tomorrows were going to look like; she didn't know if she had many tomorrows left. And yet, whenever I received any kind of text, e-mail, or call, she spoke about the promises she found in Scripture about God's eternal love, his everlasting compassion, his mercy and grace, and his perfect love for his children. It was amazing. In the midst of terrible physical suffering, she reflected an other-worldly peace in the perfect plan of God for her life.

My hope is that I will never forget the example my friend set for me. I never want to forget that in living in this perfectly imperfect world where suffering has become commonplace, my inner well-being and peace are not dependent on my circumstances. Rather, my peace (or my lack thereof) is in large part dependent on my decision to fall in line (or not) with the perfect plan that God has for me and to trust him day by day. God help us one and all to believe the truth that God loves us so much that whatever he has planned for our tomorrows will be filled with good things, because he said so.

Take-away Action Thought

When I start to worry about my unknown tomorrows, I will counter those faithless thoughts with faith-driven ones. I will call to mind this verse that reminds me of who God promises to be for me and what he promises to fill my life with: "For the LORD God is a sun and shield; the LORD bestows favor and honor; no good thing does he withhold from those whose walk is blameless" (Psalm 84:11).

My Heart's Cry to You, O Lord

Father, please help me to rest in the knowledge that you are my sun and shield, that you promise to bestow favor and honor on me, and that no matter how dire some situations may appear from my limited human perspective, you alone know what is best for me. I thank you for placing deep within my heart and soul a knowing confidence that you are always with me, thinking about me, and hearing my pleas for help, and that you will never give up on me. While it's true that none of us can know the future, we can know you! That, in truth, is all we need to know. Amen.

Giving Thanks for My Perfectly Imperfect Life

1. This week, I will take pen to paper and begin prayerfully writing down anything and everything that causes me to lose my peace. No matter if it's a person, place, or thing, I will record whatever God brings to my heart and mind. Then, I will hand each of these worries back into the care and keeping of God, one by one.

2. Because I know that my future is in the hands of the Lord and that he promises to be my sun and shield, I will pray with a thankful heart for all that he is still going to do in and through me. I'll write in my journal any insights God gives me as I take time to sit in silent adoration of him and focus on his unchanging character and how comforting this timeless truth is for every one of his children.

3. When I next feel as though God is not allowing or is withholding something good from me, I will stop and say this verse out loud. I will, by faith, thank God for protecting me and pursuing me and perfecting me through life's ups and downs. I will prayerfully commit myself to living one day at a time and to not getting ahead of myself or God. I'll patiently wait on God to direct me and fulfill his perfect plan for me.

Chapter 5

Perfectly Imperfect—Our Spiritual Maturity

"God opposes the proud
but shows favor to the humble."
1 Peter 5:5 (from Proverbs 3:34)

In every respect we are dependent upon God to enable us and prosper our efforts. We must depend upon God to do for us what we cannot do for ourselves. We must, to the same degree, depend on Him to enable us to do what we must do for ourselves.

Jerry Bridges

Melanie stood hunched over her kitchen sink, snapping green beans from her garden for all she was worth. Her brisk pace of alternately snapping, washing, and chopping her garden beans would surely counter her dark mood as she completed this task with skill and speed. Or so she hoped. Everyone who was acquainted with Melanie knew her for her quick wit and sharp comebacks. Melanie loved the Lord with all of her heart, but there were times—more times than she liked to admit—that some not so subtle verbal stabs at those around her occasionally laced her quick wit and sharp comebacks. After verbal slip-ups of the unkind variety, Melanie always felt the Holy Spirit's gentle rebuke inside her heart and mind; and to her credit, Melanie was swift to ask for forgiveness.

The only exception to Melanie's ask-for-pardon-fast rule was when she and her daughter, Jayne, became entangled in a misunderstanding or disagreement. Melanie's characteristic lightning-fast responses only served to upset her quiet, thought-ful daughter. For her part, Jayne felt like she needed to summon up her courage whenever she needed to broach a topic with her mom. Jayne often silently prayed a brief request for divine help whenever she and her mom needed to make a decision or talk through an impasse. Melanie was well aware that Jayne felt anxious before they talked, but that realization ironically served to make Melanie all the more assertive and impatient. *Why can't my own daughter understand that I only want what is best for her?* Melanie lamented inwardly, snapping the beans as fast as she possibly could. *I'm not trying to undermine Jayne or hurt her in any way, but she is so sensitive.*

And there it was: Melanie with her heightened sense of urgency to communicate as quickly and as passionately as possible; and Jayne, whose own communication style traveled slowly along the lines of peace at all costs—which meant that never the twain would meet.

Lately, however, Melanie started asking a good friend, Joan, to keep her accountable in both her attitude and her words. Joan, who was Melanie's opposite in every way, related more to Jayne than to Melanie, which made for the perfect friend to help Melanie stay on track in her communication efforts.

But on this particular afternoon of bean preparation, Mela-nie was not in the mood for anyone to speak truth into her life. She already felt the sting of failure after yet another frustrating conversation with Jayne. "I thought I had been doing so much better holding my thoughts, listening quietly, and not giving unasked-for advice," Melanie cried out in frustration as she put down the beans. "But this afternoon, it all blew up in my face again. I give up. I'm done trying. Nothing is working with Jayne."

While Melanie lamented her inadequacies in none too quiet a fashion, Jayne heard her mom's frantic prep work in the kitchen from her bedroom upstairs—as well as her words.

Listening to her mom, especially her despairing words said aloud to no one in particular, somehow softened Jayne's heart. *She did try to hold back and listen more today,* Jayne thought to herself. *And Mom didn't strong-arm me into her way of thinking either. Even though the conversation didn't end well, I guess we made some progress. Maybe I need to tell her I see that?* After saying a brief prayer for divine help, Jayne went downstairs to the kitchen. Walking over to her mom, she put her hand on her shoulder and said, "Mom, we need to talk. And before you say anything, I want you to know how much I love and respect you. And I want you to know that I appreciate how hard you're trying to communicate with me in a way that works for me."

Melanie could tell that Jayne's words were sincere. "Oh, Jayne," Melanie said through tears. "You don't know how much that means to me. I am trying to change. But you know I'm a slow work in progress!"

There's God's part and then there's our part. Sometimes we get discouraged when we know the right thing to do—or say—and then we do or say just the opposite. Melanie understood herself well. She recognized that her mode of conversing often fell into the categories of hurtful or harmful. She wanted to change and she was serious enough about growing in her spiritual maturity that she asked a good friend to keep her accountable. While these are all wonderful intentions, Melanie didn't take into account that even though she desired to be spiritually mature, this didn't mean she would ever be perfect.

Isn't it at that same imperfect fork in the road where most of us give up? We want to change and grow. We do our best to put God-honoring principles into practice. We even ask our close friends to help keep us on track, to keep us accountable so we don't give up. But when we fail it hurts all the more because of the intentional prayer and efforts we've extended to get it right (perfect!). Like Melanie, we also fail to take into account that we will fail again and again and again—but that we will grow. We will grow in spiritual maturity, as we humble ourselves under the mighty helping hand of God by asking for forgiveness and then stepping back up to try again.

Let's never forget God's formula for giving his people the grace to keep growing. It's all about humility. "God opposes the proud but shows favor to the humble." What more can we ask for? God's favor will rest on us all the days of our lives, as we continue to pursue him in humility and holiness.

 Take-away Action Thought

When I fail again (and I will), instead of giving up in despair because of my imperfection, I will humble myself before God's mighty hand and ask for forgiveness. Then I will offer thanks to God for his untiring willingness to continue sanctifying me all the days of my life. My focus will always be on God rather than on my own failings, weaknesses, and imperfections.

My Heart's Cry to You, O Lord

Father, I blew it again. I'm so frustrated with my lack of growth. I know my weaknesses and my sinful tendencies better than anyone except you. I thought I was making progress in overcoming these areas where I struggle so much. But today I proved that theory wrong again. Please forgive me for falling into the same old bad habits and giving in to my sinful desires. I want to do better, and if I'm honest, I want to conquer these tendencies and never deal with them again. But that isn't going to happen, is it? Sure, I'll grow and have some success . . . but perfection? Never. Not here on earth. Please help me to keep pressing ahead day by day, doing my part (my imperfect best), while you do your part to change me from the inside out. Amen.

Giving Thanks for My Perfectly Imperfect Life

1. I will write down every area of struggle in which I am trying to grow. I'll review each area of weakness and make note of specific situations where I seem to find it the most difficult to respond and act with spiritual maturity.

2. As I pray about these areas where I don't believe I'm growing spiritually, I will ask God to help me form a game plan. I will pray about what triggers my poor reactions or sinful tendencies, and search for Bible verses that address those specific challenges.

3. This week I will contact a close friend and share my struggles. I will then ask this person to keep me accountable and to encourage me when I feel like giving up. I will remind myself that my goal isn't perfection—but growth in grace and spiritual maturity.

 Chapter 6

Perfectly Imperfect—Our Hopes, Dreams, and Desires

So Christ himself gave the apostles, the prophets, the
evangelists, the pastors and teachers, to equip his people
for works of service, so that the body of Christ may be
built up until we all reach unity in the faith and in
the knowledge of the Son of God and become mature,
attaining to the whole measure of the fullness of Christ.
Ephesians 4:11–13

*Anchor your heart to the character of God. Your boat will
rock. Moods will come and go. Situations will fluctuate. But
will you be left adrift on the Atlantic of despair? No, for you
have found a contentment that endures the storm. No more
"if only." . . . Replace your "if only" with "already." Look
what you already have. Treat each anxious thought with
a grateful one, and prepare yourself for a new day of joy.*
Max Lucado

K yra sat listening to her pastor speak on finding your joy-
ous place of ministry in the local church. He carefully
went through the passage in Ephesians 4, explaining

how God created every person with a gift, which when put into use would help them fit together with the rest of the body of Christ to form a strong, stable, ministering, and effective church. Kyra wanted to groan. Instead, she fidgeted with pen in hand and tried to stay tuned in to the remainder of the teaching. Try as she might, however, she wasn't gleaning much from her pastor's message. Her heart was just too preoccupied and discouraged to truly hear what her pastor was saying this morning.

In her mind, she was replaying a recent conversation with the lead women's ministry director, who—from Kyra's perspective—was developing the women's program at an ineffective snail's pace. Kyra's day job was project manager at an architectural firm in the city, so from experience, she understood how essential it is to see the big picture of a project before you begin. Every project, she would tell those under her supervision at the firm, first needs a vision. Not an impractical, let's-hope-against-hope idea, but one that has been thought through, talked about, and studied from every vantage point. While Kyra knew that not everyone was committed to details like she was, she was still astounded at this director's seemingly lackadaisical attitude toward the in-the-works women's program.

While she tried not to appear pushy or like someone who questioned this leader's authority, Kyra was frustrated beyond measure after every meeting. With her giftedness in planning, leading, and organization, she felt her insides flip upside down whenever she listened to this director's impractical solutions to the women's ministry's needs. *I know I have something by way of experience and giftedness to offer our women's program,* thought Kyra. *What I don't know is how to share what I know without sounding like a know-it-all.*

As the teaching concluded that Sunday morning and the worship leader and his team began playing, Kyra suddenly realized something. *Maybe, just possibly, God wants me to be willing to sit around the table with the ministry leader and her team. Maybe, just possibly, God wants me to be thankful for the interaction I have had thus far and not jump ahead of them or myself. Maybe, just possibly, God knows I can learn some important lessons from these women over time by simply paying attention. Maybe? Just possibly?* Kyra smiled to herself. *Certainly. Yes. Message received loud and clear, Lord.*

Maybe? Just possibly? We are all a lot like Kyra in that we have this perfect plan or idea we just know will benefit everyone we want to impact. But then we get involved only to discover there's another plan already in place. Splat! There go our hopes, dreams, and desires. Like Kyra, we may have life and work experiences we would love to put into play at our local church, but somehow others aren't on board with our ideas or our vision for ministry. Kyra is to be commended for wanting to use the gifts God has given her for the benefit of others, because there are far too many Sunday-morning-only Christians who do not even consider their obligation to serve fellow believers within the church.

What Kyra didn't understand at the outset was that as gifted in planning, leading, and organization as she was, those qualifications didn't mean she was free to "take the reins" and "take over," tempting though it might be to someone as multitalented as Kyra. Instead, God allowed her to be part of the whole. While Kyra's gifts and talents may go unused for a season or two within the framework of that particular women's ministry, God would most certainly not be idle in her life.

We need to continually remind ourselves that God never wastes anything. Kyra slowly came to understand that truth and, while her exciting plans for a dynamic women's program may not come to fruition today, God was busy developing much needed fruit within Kyra's heart and soul.

True enough, it can be hard to step aside or slow down to accommodate the pace of those with whom you are working on a project. It surely won't be perfect from any perspective. It can be a fruitful season of life, however, as each member of Christ's body learns to love one another, work peaceably together, and place others and their preferences before their own. Paul says in Ephesians that the outcomes of working together as the body of Christ will help us to "reach unity in the faith and in the knowledge of the Son of God and become mature, attaining to the whole measure of the fullness of Christ." Those attainments are in and of themselves worthy of our best effort and our best attitudes.

 Take-away Action Thought

When I begin to feel frustrated or even irritated that my hopes, dreams, or desires are not coming to fruition, I will increase my thankfulness quotient and begin saying "Thank you, Lord" for every possible positive aspect of my projects at work, at home, and in ministry. My ultimate aim is to have a godly and content heart, no matter the circumstances. Even if my personally held ideas never get past vision stage, I will pray for peace, unity, and a strong, stable, ministering, and effective body of Christ.

My Heart's Cry to You, O Lord

Father, I'm feeling frustrated again. I get all pumped up and excited about a new idea I just know will be well received and powerfully life changing, but then I slowly deflate when I realize that others have their own wonderful ideas of how things should be planned and carried out. In these instances, help me to be gracious and teachable. Help me to move in your timetable, Lord, and not my own. Help me to hone a content and thankful heart for wherever and with whomever you place me during this season of service. Above all, help me to deeply value a unified, peaceable community of mature believers who are full of the knowledge of you. Amen.

Giving Thanks for My Perfectly Imperfect Life

1. Today, I will spend time writing down what I believe are my God-given areas of giftedness. Then I will ask a close family member or friend to either confirm (or deny) these areas from having watched me over time as I served in the church and in my home and workplace.

2. Next, I'll write out the different positions or places of service I have held within my local church or in parachurch ministry positions. I'll prayerfully consider which tasks I most enjoyed and thrived in doing. Then, I will circle the top two ministry experiences I most valued.

3. I will seek out my pastor or someone on staff who is in charge of ministries within my local church, and inquire about current needs. Then, I'll prayerfully consider where I might best serve according to my giftedness. I will prioritize developing a content and thankful heart above seeing my own hopes, dreams, and desires realized.

 Chapter 7

Perfectly Imperfect—Our Relationships

"And when you stand praying, if you hold anything
against anyone, forgive them, so that your Father
in heaven may forgive you your sins."
Mark 11:25

*If we as believers persist in unforgiveness, our hearts are
forced to wrestle with the fact that our actions amount to
disobedience. Forgiveness is not a take-or-leave option that
only a super-Christian should be expected to take. Yes, it's
unnatural. It's supernatural. At times it's almost unbelievable.*

Nancy Leigh DeMoss

Melissa stood next to her husband, Craig, waiting for their pastor to call their names. As Melissa looked up at the large screen overhead, she could see with stunning clarity the faces of every individual being baptized that Sunday morning. Holding back her own tears of thankfulness, Melissa listened closely to each person's taped testimony that preceded their baptism in front of the entire congregation. *I never would have imagined Craig and I would be standing here today,* Melissa thought. *Just three months ago, I had given up on him and his ability to recover, and if I'm honest, I had given up on our marriage too. It is only by the grace of God that we are standing here today and ready to be baptized!*

As Melissa listened to the stories that each man, woman, and child shared on the big screen explaining why they wanted to be baptized at this time, Melissa thought about her own answer to that question. *No doubt it's because I am seeing this season as a brand-new start in our lives and in our marriage in particular.* Melissa considered the events that had unfolded over the past several months, first with Craig's stroke that precipitated another mental breakdown.

Over the many years of their married life, he had struggled with mental illness, and Melissa had been necessarily forced to pick up the pieces due to his inability to cope with life's responsibilities.

She had lost count of the number of times Craig had gone on secret spending binges, maxing out their credit cards and overdrawing their checking and savings accounts. When in the throes of his illness, he was also known to disappear for days at a time and then reappear with little memory of where he had been. Many of their family and mutual friends urged Melissa to leave Craig and divorce him. But she was convinced that she needed to stay the course, and so she stayed. While leaving Craig wasn't an option, she did battle with forgiving him for the havoc he caused.

And no wonder. Each time Craig suffered a mental breakdown, it tore Melissa and their life apart. She would do her best to make amends and rebuild whatever (and with whomever) Craig had hurt while in one of his seasons of severe illness. She loved him and was convinced he loved her as well. She remembered what her biblical counselor told her when Melissa confessed how difficult it was to forgive Craig for the destruction he caused in the aftermath of a breakdown. *I have to separate Craig from his actions. I can love Craig. I need to forgive Craig. But I can hate what he does when his mind isn't functioning right.*

On that basis, Melissa and Craig learned how to forgive and rebuild and start over. Her hope for a fresh start for him and their marriage is a bright one. He finally found the medical support he needed and then joined a group of fellow believers with similar struggles, where they could come alongside him for encouragement and accountability. Melissa also joined a women's group through their church for the help and support she so needed. No more attempts at trying to live the Christian life as solitary believers. They now understand that new hope and healing are possible for them as individuals and as a married couple. On this momentous occasion when Melissa and Craig told their church family their story and why they wanted to be baptized, it was a day of fresh starts and new beginnings.

When I listened to Melissa tell her story and her decision to be baptized along with her husband, I kept thinking of the refrain, "But God. But God. But God." Meaning what? But God had a different ending for their heartbreaking story. Satan meant it for evil, but God transformed their suffering into something beautiful for the world to behold. In a day when we are so accustomed to throwing away relationships, Melissa's commitment to honor her marriage vows despite the suffering she endured is remarkable. But Melissa is honest enough to tell anyone who will listen that even now that Craig is in a good place mentally and they are both finding solid support through friends and believers, it's not perfect. It never will be.

Sure, Craig is doing well and working again. He is fully committed to taking the best possible care of himself spiritually, mentally, emotionally, and physically. But they both realize that the stroke precipitated a breakdown no one saw coming. Melissa and Craig live with a certain measure of uncertainty, given Craig's past history and struggles with mental health.

Melissa chuckled as she remembered an awkward conversation she had with a woman from her church who seemed in awe of her deep commitment to forgive and work through her marital challenges. "I explained that learning how to forgive was a big part of learning to love Craig," she said. "But I reminded her that Craig also has to forgive me in order to truly love me. Forgiveness and love go both ways in a marriage. Forgiveness is integral in any relationship. And I'm no super saint; I have plenty of flaws, weaknesses, and imperfections too!"

Although their struggles may be more visible than most, in many ways Melissa and Craig are no different from any other married couple who learn early on that forgiveness plays a huge role in making a marriage work. Certainly, their particular challenges are unique to them, but the gospel's command to those who call themselves Christian is to forgive.

Melissa was so grateful on that Sunday morning when she waited her turn to be baptized, grateful that she could honestly walk into the water knowing full well she was forgiven by Christ and made clean. She was equally thankful that she had forgiven Craig and in her eyes he had been made clean as well. "And when you stand praying, if you hold anything against anyone, forgive them, so that your Father in heaven may forgive you your sins."

 Take-away Action Thought

When I start to harbor unforgiveness and bitterness because I'm expecting perfection from someone, I will quickly confess my sin to God. Then I will meditate on verses that speak on forgiveness and how forgiveness is not an option but a direct command from God. I will pray and ask God to help me to have reasonable expectations of others, not impossible ones.

My Heart's Cry to You, O Lord

Father, help me to never forget that refusing to forgive is not an option for me; forgiveness is a direct command. I want you to forgive me. I need to forgive others. There isn't any in-between gray area on forgiveness. But you and I both know that I struggle to forgive when I have been wronged. I feel as though I have to keep pardoning the same sinful or irresponsible behavior time after time. Please, Lord, give me a sense of urgency in the matter of forgiveness, so that I cannot rest until I have forgiven another or sought forgiveness. I want to live free of any anger or bitterness. Help me to honor you by making forgiveness my first and best response. Amen.

Giving Thanks for My Perfectly Imperfect Life

1. Today, I will write down the name of anyone I believe I have not forgiven. Then I will prayerfully go through my list and ask the Lord for the grace to fully forgive. If there are conversations I need to have with some people, I will set up times to talk. If there is restitution to be made, I will

take the steps to make it happen. I will obey the Lord and forgive with no expectations.

2. Once I have prayerfully considered if I need to forgive anyone and have obeyed the Lord to forgive, I will take time to think about anyone whom I may need to ask for forgiveness. I will ask God to bring to my heart and mind anyone I may have hurt or offended. Then I will go to that person and ask for their forgiveness.

3. Having forgiven and asked for forgiveness, I will now prayerfully ask the Lord to reveal to my heart if I am harboring unrealistic expectations of the people in my life. Do I have expectations for myself that border on perfection? Do I expect others to be perfect? I will ask the Lord to search my heart and mind and show me if I have any self-centered or self-focused attitudes that hinder my ability to love others unconditionally.

 Chapter 8

Perfectly Imperfect—Our
Vocations and God's Provision

They spoke against God; they said, "Can God really spread
a table in the wilderness? True, he struck the rock, and
water gushed out, streams flowed abundantly, but can he
also give us bread? Can he supply meat for his people?"
When the LORD heard them, he was furious; his fire broke
out against Jacob, and his wrath rose against Israel, for
they did not believe in God or trust in his deliverance.

Psalm 78:19–22

It is just as important to trust God as it is to obey Him.
When we disobey God we defy His authority and despise
His holiness. But when we fail to trust God we doubt His
sovereignty and question His goodness. In both cases we cast
aspersions upon His majesty and His character. God views our
distrust of Him as seriously as He views our disobedience.

Jerry Bridges

When Beth and Ellie first heard that their grandparents were moving into a retirement home and wanted to sell the family farmhouse (preferably to family)

45

with its five acres of woods, older sister Beth persuaded Ellie to join her in the venture. This "venture" meant quitting their respective jobs and relocating from their city in the southern part of the state. Ellie was an elementary school teacher who quickly got hired in a local school system near her grandparents' farm. Beth was a middle sales manager at her company who offered to relocate her north as well.

Both sisters decided to make the two hour move up north to first rent and renovate and then buy their grandparents' home. Beth explained to Ellie that if either of them decided after a year that she wasn't happy living on the farm, the other sister would buy back her portion of the farm. Beth was so excited about how wonderfully the renovations were coming along. What she hadn't counted on was how different her new staff members were at this location of her company. She had assumed that since she wasn't changing companies, only zip codes, her sales management position would mirror the one in the southern area of the state.

But where she was used to a hardworking and ambitious staff, Beth found her new colleagues to be much more laid-back in meeting their monthly quotas, which reflected in their paychecks and hers. Beth therefore worked diligently, setting a high standard in work ethics, and she tried to get her employees motivated to do the same. Before she moved, she had calculated on receiving the same salary plus sales bonuses, just as she had previously. Even her upper management assured her not to worry about losing any wages; they believed in Beth's ability to run her new team successfully, because she had done so in the past.

Three months after their move, Beth still hadn't broken even financially, much less increased what she had made before in her wages. Every day, she cried out to the Lord for help and faith and courage. "I'm doing all I can, Lord. I need you to step in and make up the difference. Please!" Beth prayed to and from work every day. Each evening, Beth and Ellie discussed their workdays as they prepared dinner and then tackled the next task on their renovation project list. Ellie tried to encourage her sister, but she couldn't guarantee that her coworkers would step up and work harder. No one could. But Ellie did remind Beth about the eternal truth that God had promised to meet her every need. To which, Beth would say, "Yes, but . . ." To which Ellie retorted with sisterly authority, "There are no buts when it comes to God's promises. You know that. Now start thanking the Lord even before his provision comes in." "Okay," Beth answered with resolve. "I will exercise my faith muscles starting now. And I'll start by writing down everything I am grateful for in my journal before bed tonight." And she did.

Isn't it a relatively simple matter to watch a situation such as Beth and Ellie's from afar and feel certain that God will come through for them? Believing that God had opened the door for them to purchase their grandparents' home at a greatly reduced market price, Beth and Ellie were similarly confident that God had orchestrated that generous offer. Believing that God had also given both sisters employment in their respective vocational pursuits convinced them that he was opening the way for them to make the move. Everything from doors opening to job offers to wise counsel from family and friends, who all agreed this would be a great opportunity, further cemented Beth and Ellie's decision to move.

But then what happened? The sisters uprooted and moved, still confident of God's leading and provision. Their trust in God didn't waver. They knew what he had done to get them this far and how everything had been perfect all along the way. Then real life with its glaring imperfections settled on the scene, and Beth started doubting that God would "make up the difference," as she put it in her prayers. Beth began to feel discouraged and worn down by the hard reality that the money she counted on wasn't coming in week by week. It didn't matter how hard she worked; she was also dependent on the work that needed to be accomplished by a whole team of fellow employees. Through this, she became keenly aware that she was not in control and that she had to trust in God alone for her provision.

Again, how easy for onlookers to be tempted to say to Beth, "Wait and see. God will do something that only he is able to orchestrate." But Beth, like us in similar situations where we've stepped out and obeyed God's directives and then the walls fall in on us, struggled to see past the harsh realities of her imperfect situation. Like Beth, we need to understand that God expects our trust in him in the same measure as our obedience to him—although it's never easy. Thankfully for Beth, she had a like-minded sister in Ellie, who gently encouraged her to begin (and end) her day by giving thanks for God's perfect provision (in his time and in his own way). And perhaps most important, Ellie challenged Beth to start exercising her faith muscles by thanking God for his perfect provision before she received it. Ellie knows (as does Beth) that God will provide everything we need. Beth (like you and me) just needed a friendly reminder of that eternal truth.

Take-away Action Thought

When I step out in faith in obedience to God and then difficulties start to arise, I will continue to put the full weight of my trust in him by thanking him for his perfect provision, *before* I receive what I need.

My Heart's Cry to You, O Lord

Father, I am going to begin my prayer by giving thanks for your always-perfect provision to me. You alone know what I need most in my life. On some days, I require material goods to sustain me. On other days, I am in need of lessons in trusting you to provide these material goods. Please help me today to trust you for the lack that is in my life today. I believe that I stepped out in faith and obeyed you, but now I'm struggling to trust you. I need an extra measure of grace to steady myself through this storm. I want to please you by obeying and trusting you in equal measure, come what may. Amen.

Giving Thanks for My Perfectly Imperfect Life

1. God desires that I both obey him and trust him in equal measure. I will spend some quiet moments reading and rereading this passage from Psalm 78:19–22, allowing the weight of its truth to sink into my heart and mind.

2. Today, I will thoughtfully sit before the Lord and ask him to reveal to me specific times when I obeyed him but then troubles and uncertainty came, and I was tempted to doubt his perfect provision for me.

3. I will write down the difficult situations I find myself in today. Then I will work through each situation and begin thanking God for his perfect provision amid what I consider imperfect conditions. I will stand on the truth that God has promised to meet my every need, and I will give thanks, by faith, for that perfect provision before I receive it.

 Chapter 9

Perfectly Imperfect—Our Living Environment

Who is wise and understanding among you? Let them show
it by their good life, by deeds done in the humility that
comes from wisdom. But if you harbor bitter envy and selfish
ambition in your hearts, do not boast about it or deny the
truth. . . . But the wisdom that comes from heaven is first of
all pure; then peace-loving, considerate, submissive, full of
mercy and good fruit, impartial and sincere. Peacemakers
who sow in peace reap a harvest of righteousness.

James 3:13–14, 17–18

*It does require the supernatural grace of God to live
twenty-four hours of every day as a saint, going through
drudgery, and living an ordinary, unnoticed, and ignored
existence as a disciple of Jesus. It is ingrained in us that
we have to do exceptional things for God—but we do
not. We have to be exceptional in the ordinary things of
life, and holy on the ordinary streets, among ordinary
people—and this is not learned in five minutes.*

Oswald Chambers

Rachel looked outside her kitchen window to the spacious and stunningly lush hillside that swept like a green canopy to the lakeshore. One of the best features of this lake house was this view, Rachel recalled lovingly. She still remembered how their savvy realtor gently steered her toward that spectacular scene. Peaceful. Tranquil. Perfect. Truly gorgeous by anyone's standards. Whenever she stood at that window preparing food or cleaning up afterward, she lingered for a few extra moments, drinking in the loveliness of God's creation. "Oh Lord," Rachel whispered. "What a perfect picture of your handcrafted beauty."

Sadly, those peaceful interludes never lasted long enough. Truth be told, the only time her house enjoyed peace and quiet was when Rachel was alone. Between her husband, Matt, and their three almost grown and gone young adult children, her home life was anything but happy or hospitable. Try as she might to set a godly example as both a wife and a mom, she had an uphill battle day in and day out.

Rachel had made a personal and public commitment to Christ only a few years earlier. Matt didn't care too much about these changes in Rachel's life, until she began to beg off from the parties and weekend barhopping that had been a pattern since they married. Her kids didn't take much notice either, until she said no to questionable movies, concerts, and television programs. Then the day came when the fireworks erupted, leaving Rachel feeling isolated and misunderstood with a heart that ached for her family to know Jesus' love too.

Rachel had tried her best to live out her faith through consistent acts of loving service toward her family. In the early days after her conversion, she had sat down with Matt and the children to explain her newfound faith. To their credit, they all listened respectfully, and she often looks back on those early days when she felt joyful and hopeful. Sadly, these days it was just the opposite—and now Matt and the kids asked her how long she was going to keep up this religious act. Oh, how that stung! Couldn't her family see how sincere she was? How she had changed? She certainly felt like a whole new person.

After a while, Rachel realized that no amount of persuasive conversations or timely comments was going to soften her family's heart. She could only demonstrate through her actions how God had changed her. One day at a time. One act of service at a time. One kind response to an unkind or hurtful remark at a time. One decision to forgive at a time. One prayer at a time. *While I want more than anything for Matt and the kids to come to a saving knowledge of Christ, I know that only the Holy Spirit can change a person's heart. It's my job to clothe myself in humility and love and to pray without ceasing. And I will!*

As Rachel discovered, there is no outward material blessing that can temper the harshness of living with those who are hostile to our faith. While she had expected some pushback from her family after she first committed her life to Christ, she had been surprised to receive very little of that from them. It wasn't until the inside-out transformation in Rachel's heart and mind and lifestyle began to affect her family's sinful choices and preferences that they balked. While Matt and the kids couldn't fault Rachel for what she chose to do (or not do), it rankled them when her personal convictions and presence began to interrupt *their* lives.

Thankfully, Rachel had received some wise advice from a fellow believer soon after she became a Christian, which now came to her mind as she pondered what to do about her family. Her friend had already been down the same path, so she counseled her to tread lightly with how much she tried to push for change or persuade her family to turn to Christ. "Speak when you can whenever God opens the door," she had shared, "but put the bulk of your efforts into growing and maturing yourself—and love them, just love them. Let the Holy Spirit do the wrestling within your family's hearts. Make sense?" Rachel nodded. "Love them. Love them," she now prayed at that kitchen window, looking out at the hopeful horizon. "That, Lord, will be my perfectly imperfect plan: to simply love them."

 ## Take-away Action Thought

When I begin to feel discouraged and want to give up because those close to me do not share my faith, I will find a quiet place and reflect on this passage in James 3. I'll re-dedicate myself to personal growth in holiness. I will focus on God's promises to me, and I will purpose to humbly serve my family and meet their needs in every way I can.

My Heart's Cry to You, O Lord

Father, I am feeling so disheartened. I'm struggling against discouragement and the temptation to give up on my family ever coming to a saving relationship with Jesus. I'm doing my best to love and serve them in every way possible. I am honestly giving my all to them through service and by caring for them day by day. And yet, there is so much dissension in our house. I have no one on my side. No one understands me or my faith. Please help me to stay at the task and not grow weary of doing good. Help me to focus on who you are to me and how you have promised to meet my every need. Lord, make the fruits of the Spirit so evident in my life that my family can't deny this supernatural transformation. Amen.

Giving Thanks for My Perfectly Imperfect Life

1. I will spend time reading and meditating on this passage from James 3, and I will prayerfully ask the Lord to grow these godly qualities into my life. I will write these character qualities down on cards and consider how I might love my family by displaying them.

2. Prayerfully, I will ask the Lord to show me any areas in which I'm exhibiting a prideful, resentful, or argumentative spirit. Instead, I will ask the Lord to clothe me with humility, forgiveness, and peace.

3. This week, I will contact several fellow believers and enlist their prayer for me to be sensitive to God's leading as I serve my family. And I will ask them to intercede for my family members as well. To help keep me accountable and encouraged, I will keep my friends updated on my progress.

 Chapter 10

Perfectly Imperfect—Our Leisure Activities

And whatever you do, whether in word or deed,
do it all in the name of the Lord Jesus, giving
thanks to God the Father through him.

Colossians 3:17

If you're sitting down to dinner, be thankful.
If you're getting up to go to bed, be thankful.
If you're coming out from under a two-week cold and cough,
if you're paying bills,
if you're cleaning up after overnight company,
if you're driving to work,
if you're changing a light bulb,
if you're worshiping in a church service,
if you're visiting a friend in the hospital,
if you're picking up kids from school or practice . . .
be thankful. God has commanded it—
for our good and for His glory.
Nancy Leigh DeMoss

Annie sat with her three closest friends at their favorite downtown coffee shop, as they passed around the colorful brochures of tropical cruise destinations. Annie's friend, Esther, was turning forty and decided she wanted to celebrate in style. Although Annie would love to go on a cruise, her paycheck didn't stretch far enough for such an expensive vacation. As the others discussed the trip, she puzzled to herself, *Isn't this why the four of us all invested in camping gear over the past five years . . . to save money on vacations? So why aren't we here planning our yearly camping trip? Where did the idea of taking a cruise even come from?*

It wasn't that she thought a cruise wouldn't be a fantastic change of pace, especially since Esther wanted to celebrate her birthday in a grander way this year. Annie simply couldn't justify the expense. If she agreed to go, then she would be forced to dip into her savings, which is something she wouldn't do. She didn't want to put a damper on her three friends' enthusiastic daydreams about which luxurious cruise to schedule, but she knew she had to be up-front with her decision before they went any further on this idea.

"Ah, hey," she said, "I would love to go on a cruise with you all, but I really can't afford it right now. But go ahead and make the reservations before the cruise ship books up." "What!" Esther cried loud enough that those seated nearby looked over. "You aren't coming with us?"

"Esther, I don't have the money for a vacation like this. And I'm not dipping into my savings for it. I'm saving for my next car. You know the one I'm driving now is old, and I need to buy another one sooner rather than later. I'm sorry." Suddenly they were all quiet. The four friends didn't really know what to say next. When the awkward silence continued, Annie felt tempted to jump up and leave.

After what seemed like forever, Annie's friends started to talk at the same time. "We'll figure something out. Don't feel bad. Let's look around at our camping options again. I can't really afford a cruise either to be honest." She looked from face to face, as her friends responded like the true friends they were. Annie felt grateful. She may not be able to travel to picture-perfect distant locales, but she didn't need to go far in search of loyal and loving friends who were priceless.

The irony of life is this: Even when we think we have established a perfect solution to a problem, life has a way of dispersing our little plans into a million pieces. Annie and her friends had agreed years earlier that since they were blessed to live near the mountains and they all loved hiking and camping, rather than spend money none of them had on pricey vacations out of state, they would vacation in state. So they did. For the past five years, the four friends had set up a series of vacation planning coffee dates when they would decide on their destination, assess what they needed for camping gear and supplies, and then divide the expenditures four ways. It was perfect. Until it wasn't.

Thankfully, for Annie and her three friends, they realized that their friendship and spending time together was more valuable than one or two of them setting off on their own just to experience something new. These four friends had long ago set aside this one week in the summer to get away—together. They were committed to keeping their yearly tradition going for as long as possible.

In a perfect world, folks could go where they wanted when they wanted with whom they wanted. But in our imperfect, real world, we all have choices to make. Annie was wise enough to politely say no, giving her friends the opportunity to choose what they wanted to do—which was to stick together.

But Annie understood that if she had gone against her better judgment just to go along with her friends, there would have been a price to pay beyond the financial cost. She was wise enough to realize that God is the owner of all things, and he sometimes (a lot of times?) uses money to help guide us, restrain us, bless us, and teach us about what matters most in life.

It's about so much more than our bank accounts. What we have (or don't have) stretches us to trust God as our perfect provider and learn to give thanks all the time, in every circumstance. Whether it's a struggle to be grateful for a two-hour walk in the woods or a once-in-a-lifetime overseas trip, God wants our hearts to be thankful. He wants us to be able to express that supernatural response, no matter what we are doing (or aren't able to do). It really doesn't matter what our circumstances are if we are committed to surrendering ourselves (and all we have) to our loving Lord's sovereign care and keeping. As Nancy Leigh DeMoss wrote, "Be thankful. God has commanded it—for our good and for His glory."

 Take-away Action Thought

I will choose to give thanks even when, especially when, my expectations are dashed or when I want something I do not have. I will purpose to give thanks first thing in the morning and the last thing at night—and all the hours in between.

My Heart's Cry to You, O Lord

Father, I feel as though I was being tested this week. I so wanted to say yes to my friends' request to join them in their plans. But Lord, I don't have the money to spend on what they want to do. Although most of the time I accept my financial limitations, for a few hours, I admit I felt resentful to be limited in my choices because of money. I want to consistently give thanks to you for your perfect provision for me. You often meet my wants, but you always meet my needs.

Lord, help me to continue to develop a consistently grateful heart that rises up full of thanks in the morning and doesn't stop giving thanks when my head hits the pillow at night. Amen.

Giving Thanks for My Perfectly Imperfect Life

1. I will start my week by writing a gratitude list. From small to large, I will write out everything I am grateful for until I run out of things that I can think of at the moment. Then I will prayerfully review each item on my list and thoughtfully consider what my life would be like without these blessings from God.

2. Next, I will write down some hopes, dreams, and desires. I will not consider limitations, whether they are financial or pie in the sky ones. I will pray through each item and trust the Lord for every hope, dream, and desire, knowing that he withholds only those things that are not good for me or that will not bring him glory.

3. Today, I will focus on contentment. I'll memorize the passage above from Colossians and recite it when I wake up in the morning, at every meal, and when I go to bed at night. I'll then reflect on how focusing on this Scripture has helped me love my perfectly imperfect life.

 # Chapter 11

Perfectly Imperfect—Our Ministries

In him we were also chosen, having been predestined
according to the plan of him who works out everything
in conformity with the purpose of his will.

Ephesians 1:11

*No plan of God's can be thwarted; when He acts, no one
can reverse it; no one can hold back His hand or bring Him
to account for His actions. God does as He pleases, only
as He pleases, and works out every event to bring about
the accomplishment of His will. Such a bare unqualified
statement of the sovereignty of God would terrify us if
that were all we knew about God. But God is not only
sovereign; He is perfect in love, and infinite in wisdom.*

Jerry Bridges

A few years into her career, Lindsay had felt a strong sense
of calling to work with young teen girls at the juvenile
detention center in her city. Lately, however, Lindsay
had begun rethinking her plan for ministry. She felt stuck in
a confusing, emotional season right now, wondering how she
could move forward at this point after her closest friend, Kate,

committed suicide. There was so much shock and grief, Lindsay didn't know what to do with all of her emotions. So she did what many people do: she tried to ignore them, stuff them deep down inside, and stay so busy she wouldn't have time to feel them.

While Lindsay didn't turn away from her faith or her church family during that emotionally intense and depressing time, she did question how Kate, who had been her closest Christian friend and had wanted to work alongside Lindsay with the troubled teens in their area, could end her own life. As Lindsay reflected on the many conversations they had together brainstorming about this teen ministry, Lindsay wondered how she had missed the cues in Kate's life. Why hadn't she picked up on her despair? Could she have talked her dear friend out of taking her life? What had Lindsay missed?

These troubling thoughts tumbled around and around inside of Lindsay's mind as she tried to work through her grief. She then began to doubt in her ability to meet the needs of these teens—these troubled teens—if she hadn't been able to help her closest friend. *Doubt. Self-recrimination. Defeat.* These were the words that aptly described Lindsay's thoughts and emotions as she struggled with what to do. Her church was already pairing up adult women with female teens through their local church and the kick-off was this weekend. She had to make a decision.

Still unsure, Lindsay was just about to call the director of ministry and ask to be taken off the list of adult volunteers when her phone rang—and it was the director. She listened intently to the director explain that there was a high school girl whose best friend had committed suicide several weeks earlier. Knowing what Lindsay was going through over her own loss, the director felt this might be helpful—for both of them.

This changed everything for Lindsay. She now recognized that God was placing her and this hurting teen together for a reason. And while she may not have all the answers to her questions about her friend's suicide, together the two of them could travel along the same road in search of them. Lindsay felt sure that, though this wasn't the way she had wanted to enter into ministry, it was God's perfect plan and he would oversee it according to his will and eternal purpose.

How many times have we developed a passion for serving in a certain capacity and then all our enthusiasm falls flat when a real-life calamity threatens to overwhelm and undermine us, causing us to doubt what we had felt so confident about pursuing? Lindsay's loss of her dearest friend to suicide set in motion a whole range of thoughts that told her she wasn't qualified to serve troubled teens if she hadn't been able to detect the despair in her own friend's life.

Lindsay, like us, was tempted to believe that if we aren't able to prevent something horrible from happening, then we are forever disqualified from service. That is exactly where Satan wants us.

Defeated. Paralyzed. Demoralized. Hopeless.

Yet God wants us to see that even when we cannot stop a tragedy and our heart feels broken beyond repair, he is present. God is close by, tending to our deepest wounds and beginning his own restoration work within us, so that in time we will be able to help restore others. At the very cusp of giving up, Lindsay discovered God in the center of the healing process. When she received the phone call about a teen suffering as she was, she knew it was a divine appointment. Something reignited within Lindsay's heart and mind, and she knew God had placed them together for this season.

Lindsay's pain, our pain, will never be wasted if we allow the Lord to gently minister to us in our brokenness. Then, once we are strengthened, we can go out and minister that same compassion and care to others. From Lindsay's perspective, it seemed as though her plans for ministry were dashed because of personal tragedy. From God's perspective, Lindsay's ministry would flourish all the more brightly, because of what she had endured and survived. Perfectly imperfect.

 Take-away Action Thought

When I fall into doubt and confusion because what is happening is not what I had planned, I will remember that God in his sovereignty can bring hope out of the most hopeless situations, and that he can use my pain and suffering as an agent of restoration to others.

My Heart's Cry to You, O Lord

Father, I had such grand plans and was so passionate about serving others in ministry. And then, when tragedy struck, I felt confused and blindsided by my own emotions and questions. I could not understand how this could happen to someone so close to me. It shook me to my core. You know how hopeless and numb I've been feeling as I grieve. But I also am beginning to see your hand of divine orchestration, as you help me move past my pain so that I can minister to others. Help me to rely on your perfect love and infinite wisdom to bring hope and healing to whomever I am called to serve. Amen.

Giving Thanks for My Perfectly Imperfect Life

1. This week I will make note of any (and every) instance where I see God's sovereign hand working to orchestrate my ministry efforts. I'll journal any (and all) divine interactions and note how God brought me together with the right person to encourage and serve.

2. I will spend time this week in daily prayer, asking the Lord to place me exactly where I am most effective in ministry. I will prayerfully (and trustingly) ask God to guide me where I can be used as an agent of restoration and change.

3. If I am unsure about areas of service within my local church body or a parachurch ministry, I'll ask those who know me best to pray for me and to talk with me about where they believe I might be best suited. I will remind myself that even when I feel the most unqualified to serve, God's word tells us that he is the one who has fit us for service for good works before the beginning of time.

 Chapter 12

Perfectly Imperfect—Our Service to Others

Make every effort to add to your faith goodness; and to
goodness, knowledge; and to knowledge, self-control; and to
self-control, perseverance; and to perseverance, godliness;
and to godliness, mutual affection; and to mutual affection,
love. For if you possess these qualities in increasing
measure, they will keep you from being ineffective and
unproductive in your knowledge of our Lord Jesus Christ.

1 Peter 1:5–8

We are not made for the mountains . . . those are simply
intended to be moments of inspiration. We are made
for the valley and the ordinary things of life, and that
is where we have to prove our stamina and strength.

Oswald Chambers

Tabi felt as though she were stealing time as she tried to relax with a hot cup of tea while her two boys were napping. Alternately sipping and exhaling deeply, she has learned to relish these quiet moments in the early afternoons.

Like most perfectionists, she had an ambitious daily to-do list on which she labored from morning until night to finish. What an inner feeling of self-satisfaction and accomplishment she experienced on those days when she could cross off every single task she had hoped to complete. Before the children were born, she had been able to create a list that would make most folks cringe, yet she almost always had it completely finished before bedtime. These days, not so much.

Tabi felt a tad guilty of expecting too much of herself and others. *And why not?* Tabi reasoned to herself. *Even after an especially hectic day, when there's work to be done, I do it. No one can complain that I don't keep my house, our kids, and my life in efficient working order.* What she failed to reckon on was that her husband, Ryan, would much rather see her leave a few tasks undone so she could relax and enjoy being with him and their boys. It wasn't that Tabi didn't love her family. She did. From her perspective, however, every ounce of self-discipline and energy she expended on their behalf spelled out L-O-V-E in capital letters. Except when it didn't.

To Ryan and the boys, it seemed that they were more of an interruption to her than welcome company. While Tabi wanted to join them for some fun, she also knew she had to get a lot done beforehand. This was how she had been raised by her hardworking yet emotionally distant parents.

Because he was concerned, Ryan often talked with her about this internal tug-of-war she had every day: Work or play? Work or rest? Work or simply *be*? It was a battle she really wanted to win, because in her heart of hearts she knew that the best act of service to those she loved was to simply be present in the moment and love them.

Work or play? Work or rest? Work or simply be? For those of us who admit to being perfectionists, the battle Tabi fought inside of her heart and mind is a familiar one. I believe each of us sincerely desires to make the most of our days to honor Christ, and so we work hard to be both effective and productive. These are wonderful traits. We make great spouses and friends and employees, because we make sure to do our part. However—and there's always a however, right?—what we perfectionists sometimes fail to see in our service to others, especially those we love dearly, is that our loved ones desire us most. Our presence. Our full attention. Our ability to simply be with them. Not edging off our seats to go do something else that remains on the never-ending to-do list.

Perhaps one of the most difficult challenges for us perfectionists as we strive to be productive members of society is to remember to place people above our endless tasks and responsibilities. We need to invert our internal priority list and put people at the top. How? By focusing on the importance of loving those around us, especially our own families. We can start by adding to our faith goodness,

> and to goodness, knowledge; and to knowledge, self-control; and to self-control, perseverance; and to perseverance, godliness; and to godliness, mutual affection; and to mutual affection, love. For if [we] possess these qualities in increasing measure, they will keep [us] from being ineffective and unproductive in [our] knowledge of our Lord Jesus Christ.

We perfectionists must choose to grow from goodness to knowledge to self-control to perseverance to godliness to mutual affection to love.

But, you may ask, when will all the work get done? I've yet to meet a perfectionist (or a recovering perfectionist) who failed to fulfill their work responsibilities because they spent quality time with others. I have, however, met countless perfectionists (and recovering perfectionists) who struggle to prioritize people (even their beloved people) over their to-do lists. This is why I love that quotation from Oswald Chambers.

> We are not made for the mountains . . . those are simply intended to be moments of inspiration. We are made for the valley and the ordinary things of life, and that is where we have to prove our stamina and strength.

It is true. We are made for the ordinary things of life, the day-in and day-outs of life among our people. That's where we can live out in real time our mutual affection and love by serving those we love by being fully present.

 ## Take-away Action Thought

When I am tempted to prioritize my to-do list above spending time with my loved ones, I will stop and ask the Lord to help me be self-controlled enough to set aside the work for a time. I will ask the Lord to help me regain an eternal perspective on what matters most in this life: people!

My Heart's Cry to You, O Lord

Father, I have this ongoing internal battle that rages whenever I start to prioritize work over the people in my life. I feel drawn to working hard and finishing everything I start. While these are good traits to have, I also realize that I often put so much emphasis on getting my work done that I unknowingly neglect the people close to me. Help me to develop a more sensitive eternal perspective on the value of people over production. I really want to put others first and love them well by being fully present, but it doesn't come naturally to me. I need your strength and grace to let go of those perfectionist tendencies that hinder me from loving my loved ones in the way they need to be loved. Amen.

Giving Thanks for My Perfectly Imperfect Life

1. This week I will make a different type of to-do list. Instead of listing every task I want or need to accomplish, I will make a list of five ways to intentionally serve and love my family in personal ways.

2. Each day this week, I will prayerfully ask the Lord to show me new and creative ways to love my family and friends that mean the most to each of them. I will choose to communicate my love in simple, everyday ways.

3. I will also ask for prayer support from a few trusted friends to help keep me accountable with how I choose to prioritize my time spent with others. I'll also journal each evening this week and record how rewarding it was when I honored my commitment to set aside tasks in favor of time well spent with loved ones.

 Chapter 13

Perfectly Imperfect—Our Physical Bodies

And let us run with perseverance the race marked out for us,
fixing our eyes on Jesus, the pioneer and perfecter of faith.
Hebrews 12:1–2

You see, the devil always wants us to gaze upon the horizontal
circumstances of life. But God wants us to maintain that
upward look, to gaze upon Him and just occasionally glance
at our circumstances. When you are gazing on God, He
invariably gives you the strength and peace to handle those
glances at your circumstances. Conversely, when you're gazing
at your circumstances, they can literally overwhelm you with
discouragement, doubt and despair. But when you are caught
up into the awesome wonder of who God is and what He has
done, with the eyes of your heart riveted upon Him, He will
supernaturally empower you to handle anything around you!
Richard A. Burr

I was born in 1960, and by the time this book is released, I
will be sixty years old. I'm still not sure I can wrap my mind
around that number, because on the inside I feel like I'm

circling thirty-five indefinitely. Case in point: this morning as I was driving to my doctor's office for a check-up to discuss the results of my recent blood work, I heard a comment on the radio that I thought, with irony, was timed perfectly for me: "How old are you if you don't know how old you are?" What a terrific question. This is why when I considered my inner person, not my outward physical self, I answered back, "I'm thirty-five!"

For the past week or so, I've been conscious of the fact that I had to do a ten-hour fast before having my blood drawn. I've also been conscious of the fact that my cholesterol counts have been too high. Feeling edgy and distracted, I had been putting off this test for several reasons: (1) I like to drink coffee with cream first thing in the morning; (2) I know my past history with this particular test; and (3) I have a new doctor whom I respect and like very much, but we haven't had this particular conversation yet. I suddenly realized that, for me, the bottom line is that I can get too caught up and discouraged by my aging body, knowing that with every check-up the risk increases that something could be wrong with me. I call these "sneak attacks," because you can go in feeling wonderful but a blood screen or a test can reveal hidden dangers.

Like most people, my older body doesn't respond with younger me's physical resilience in terms of energy, sleep, and a host of internal slow-downs, misfirings, and illness-related risks. Being the recovering perfectionist that I am, I struggle when I consider how quickly I used to bounce back after babies, illnesses, and injuries. I feel frustrated at times, because I do attempt to eat well and exercise all throughout the week. And yet, my aging body isn't cooperating with my efforts so much. When I look at growing older (and all those age-related risks) from a horizontal perspective, I feel like giving up.

These days, when I enter my doctor's office (or my dentist's office, my ophthalmologist's office, my dermatologist's office, or my GYN's office!), I start to realize how much commitment and energy it takes to simply sustain the good health I currently enjoy—let alone try to improve it. The older I get, the more I realize that I am not in control of what God allows to happen inside of my physical body. Every day, this increasingly obvious lack-of-control reality hits me harder and harder. I'm not talking about graying hair, wrinkles, sags, and weight gain. I'm speaking of the truly life-altering, forever-debilitating type of illnesses and diseases that may come my way. But I'm slowly learning that this is much more than a physical battle, it's a spiritual one! As author Richard Burr writes, "The devil always wants us to gaze upon the horizontal circumstances of life. But God wants us to maintain that upward look, to gaze upon Him and just occasionally glance at our circumstances." I need to keep my gaze upward—and I dare say, so do you!

Quoting Richard Burr again: "When you're gazing at your circumstances, they can literally overwhelm you with discouragement, doubt and despair." I love this reminder, because I need it today and I'll need it for all my tomorrows. I want to run the particular race God has set for me with my eyes fixed on Jesus, the pioneer and perfecter of faith. I can only accomplish all that God has for me if I am consistently keeping my focus on him. Like everyone else, when I conversely allow myself to gaze endlessly at my circumstances, I do become filled with discouragement, doubt, and despair. Don't you?

Only by redirecting my heart and mind upward toward God and maintaining my focus on him will I be able to face today and my tomorrows with a preserving faith. Little by little, even my best perfectionist habits for healthy self-care will not be enough to hold back the ravages of age, illness, and disease. The older I grow, the more I'll need Jesus' continuous power, strength, and grace in order to keep running my race until he calls me home. Much of my attitude toward these changes in my physical body depends on one choice alone: What do I choose to focus on day by day when familiar tasks take more strength than they used to take? When sleep doesn't come as easily (or as soundly) as it once did? When my doctor gives me the hard news about test results I don't want to hear? What then? I will lean all more heavily on Jesus for the power, strength, and grace I need to finish the race he set before me. There's really no other way.

 ## Take-away Action Thought

When I start to feel overwhelmed by discouragement, doubt, and despair because of the physical changes or problems I'm facing in my body, I will choose to move my focus upward. I will choose to keep my gaze on God and only glance at my circumstances.

My Heart's Cry to You, O Lord

Father, please help me to wake up each morning with an attitude of thankfulness that you have given me yet another day to serve you. Help me to immediately set my focus on who you are, O Lord. When I'm not feeling strong or able, when I'm dreading all I need to accomplish that day, or when I'm just feeling tired and worn out, help me to be self-disciplined enough to keep looking upward. Give me your wisdom and grace to realize that while the circumstances of my life will most certainly alter in ways I may not like, you remain the same. You, O Lord, are my loving heavenly Father who will never let go of my hand. Amen.

Giving Thanks for My Perfectly Imperfect Life

1. Today, I will set aside an hour to be alone with the Lord. I'll ask God to help me be honest about the areas in my physical body that are hurting or are not functioning correctly or that I'm worried about. Above all, I'll be honest with the Lord about how I feel when my body doesn't work properly. Then I'll look up three verses on gratitude, write them out, and reread them several times every day.

2. I will sit with a journal in hand and write down any specific instances that come to mind when I spent too much time focusing on my circumstances instead of keeping my focus upon the Lord. I will also put on paper how God eventually worked out each situation, and I will then prayerfully contemplate how I could have suffered less emotionally and mentally if I had kept my focus on God.

3. This week, I will write down any situations in which I am tempted to set my gaze on my troubling circumstances. Instead, I will search out an appropriate Bible promise and write it next to each situation listed. Then I will begin and end my day by reviewing and meditating on God's promises of perfect provision for me. My gaze will be on God and his promises, not on my imperfect circumstances.

 # Chapter 14

Perfectly Imperfect—Our Acceptance

"My grace is sufficient for you, for my power
is made perfect in weakness."
2 Corinthians 12:9

*"Do the next thing." I don't know any simpler
formula for peace, for relief from stress and anxiety
than that very practical, very down-to-earth
word of wisdom. Do the next thing.*

Elisabeth Elliot

Jenna lay with her head on her pillow, eyes shut tight, one hand grasping the plastic bucket next to her in case her stomach decided to empty its contents again, while her other hand clenched the bedsheet. Praying for relief from the dizziness that spun her into a world of darkness, she prayed, *God, help this to stop! Please make it stop.*

After being misdiagnosed for months, she finally learned she had Meniere's disease, a disorder of the inner ear for which there currently is no cure. This meant that at any time (with no warning), an attack might start that would force her into a horizontal position for hours at a time until the tinnitus, the vertigo, and the vomiting stopped.

Jenna first realized something was wrong right after she moved to a new city, when she was still getting her bearings. She simultaneously had to deal with the stress of settling into a new home, while suffering from an unknown illness that threatened her livelihood.

As a counselor, Jenna helped clients work through their own major life challenges. A natural born counselor at heart, she was blessed to be able to do what she loved most and was most gifted at. Before meeting her clients, she would carefully prepare by refreshing herself on their past experiences and current problems, poring over the most effective biblical solutions tailored specifically for each person. She herself felt blessed to have this opportunity to invest in others' lives in such a life-altering way.

So when these unexpected vertigo attacks hit hard, and then she learned that she was also going deaf in one ear, she had legitimate concerns and questions. *How will I be able to counsel if I can't hear?* Jenna wondered. *How will I keep counseling appointments if I never know when these attacks will happen?* As she faced her uncertain future, part of her struggled with the irony and imperfection of the situation: as a counselor, Jenna needed to listen well and always be available to meet with her clients. All she could do was cry out to God, "What is going on here!"

As the weeks passed and the attacks grew more frequent and more intense, Jenna continued to pursue new medical options, feeling that her counseling career might very well be over. All the while, she continued to ask God to help her to trust him with her present condition and her future.

I recall one conversation when she threw her hands up in the air and said, "I have no clue what God is going to do, but I know I must trust him and accept whatever happens." Over time, Jenna's condition did improve to the point where her first and last thoughts of the day weren't fixated on the possibility of having another attack. One day at a time, one attack at a time, Jenna discovered that God's gift of sufficient grace isn't just an empty promise; it is one that has proven true for her.

Today, while still battling a disease that has left her deaf in one ear and sometimes keeps her from being available to meet a client, Jenna has discovered that she is a better counselor with far more compassion since having suffered from this unpredictable illness. Imperfect situation? Imperfect timing? Absolutely. Defeated and undone? Just the opposite. Jenna has learned through the fires of affliction how God's provision in every circumstance is all she needs.

When I first heard about Jenna's sudden attacks of tinnitus and vertigo, along with other debilitating side effects, I recall thinking how quickly life can change and how swiftly our world can shrink in size. Jenna understandably went through a season of disbelief and shock when she first began to suffer from these sudden attacks. Over time, however, she slowly accepted her diagnosis, along with the limitations it might eventually place on her life and livelihood. As we talked, it became obvious that God was in the midst of this trial by suffering and that he was doing something good in Jenna—something with eternal repercussions.

Week by week, Jenna and I would talk and the same biblical truth kept bubbling to the top of our conversations: God's love shows up brightest and most brilliant when the backdrop of our lives is smattered with imperfections and weaknesses. We learn to see him as our most faithful provider in these flawed situations, as we choose to accept what he allows into our lives.

Does the acceptance come easy? Never. But come it must. As Jenna learned to accept that her physical limitations might be permanent additions to her life, she realized she would not waste what little surplus energy she had in fighting against the inevitable, which would only further deplete her. Instead, she learned to live fully in spite of it.

One significant choice she made each and every day was to simply "do the next thing." Often, she felt so ill or weak from a previous attack that she was unable to accomplish much. But she could do one thing: the next thing. Some days, Jenna could do several "next things," and each day she trusted God would help her to fulfill his plan for her in that twenty-four-hour space. Day by day, Jenna found peace and acceptance in her circumstances by doing the next thing—and trusting God for the rest.

When we were children, if we felt that we were in control, then we felt safe. As children of the Most High, however, desiring control does just the opposite; as adults, we understand that control is an illusion. Living for control and safety when we know Jesus as Savior and Lord personally stunts our growth and often paralyzes us.

We can learn to accept what God allows and live contentedly, thankfully, and joyfully—accepting our perfectly imperfect situation, because God promises us that his "grace is sufficient for [us], for my power is made perfect in weakness." I wonder if any of us would choose a life governed by our own making and design over the plan so carefully given through the loving sovereignty and absolute control of our merciful God? We may never fully understand the whys of our situation, but God will always give us the grace we need to do the next thing through the strength he alone provides.

✆ Take-away Action Thought

When acceptance of a difficult situation is hard, I will settle myself down quietly before the Lord and meditate on this promise: God's grace is sufficient for me, and his power is made perfect in my weakness. That is a truth I can accept.

My Heart's Cry to You, O Lord

Father, I am struggling to understand or accept the situation I am facing. I thought I understood your plan for me at this season of my life, but now the circumstances are so confounding that I'm left wondering if I heard you at all. I sorely need your wisdom, your grace, your abiding strength. I feel undone by weakness and I feel afraid. Please help me to allow the promise of your provision and strength to sink deep within my heart and mind. Help me to discipline my heart and my thoughts to not fear but to trust in you, even when I cannot see the path ahead. Amen.

Giving Thanks for My Perfectly Imperfect Life

1. Today, I will take time to study the word *acceptance* and look up as many verses as I can find to help me better understand what this means to me as I purpose to accept my situation.

2. I will sit with pen and paper and prayerfully ask God to help me recall past difficult situations when I needed God's supernatural provision. I will list these answers to prayer and then take a few moments to thank him for his perfect care for me.

3. During the coming week, I will purposefully give thanks to God for whatever challenges I am facing, while asking him to help me recognize the good he is accomplishing in me from an eternal perspective.

 Chapter 15

Perfectly Imperfect—Our Witness

> For the grace of God has appeared that offers salvation
> to all people. It teaches us to say "No" to ungodliness
> and worldly passions, and to live self-controlled, upright
> and godly lives in this present age, while we wait for the
> blessed hope—the appearing of the glory of our great
> God and Savior, Jesus Christ, who gave himself for us to
> redeem us from all wickedness and to purify for himself
> a people that are his very own, each to do what is good.
>
> Titus 2:11–14

*You can rest, and in that rest you will find a sweetness growing
in your soul that will delight and nourish those around you.
And in every way you fail, when you fall back into patterns of
unbelief and striving, you'll find the grace to wholeheartedly
and transparently repent, knowing that your sin problem
has already been taken care of and that you are forgiven.*

Elyse Fitzpatrick

Becca laughed under her breath on the way home from
Sunday services, as she recalled her pastor saying that
a man once told him that he was a secret agent for Jesus.

That was the chief oxymoron! What earthly, or heavenly, good is it to be a Christian and keep it a secret? To intentionally keep people guessing about what matters most to you? It doesn't make sense, and then there's the obedience factor too. Jesus' command to his disciples was to go and tell, not keep hidden and silent.

Becca was happy she had something to laugh about after that not-so-nice conversation she recently had with her parents. *I'm sure my family would have preferred if I kept my faith in Christ hidden,* Becca thought to herself. *It's not even as though I'm one of those boisterous personalities that make it their mission to share their opinions with everyone they meet. No, I was careful how I shared my newfound faith in Jesus; I never pushed it on Mom and Dad. Still, in their perfect showcase world, I seem to have broken some unforgivable, unwritten law.*

Becca thought back to her privileged childhood with their estate that boasted of a horse farm with all the associated bells and whistles of not only owning horses but racing them as well. Becca had, of course, attended the best private school in the area and then went on to a private and pricey college. After two years of trying to figure out her major, Becca found her calling while volunteering at a local hospital. She decided to drop out of college and train to become a phlebotomist.

Being familiar with handling livestock and helping with the day-to-day care of the animals, she was especially eager to assist when the veterinarian made his calls. How different could it be to draw blood from people? Becca thought. She was correct. Earning her living as a phlebotomist paid the bills, just barely, but it filled Becca's soul with purpose as she interacted with dozens of men, women, and children daily.

I do so well with even the most aggravating patients at work, but when it comes to talking with my folks about anything, especially anything that matters, I blow it. Maybe it would be better if I adopted the secret agent Christian persona when I'm around my folks. They hate that I didn't finish college. They hate my job choice. They hate that I refuse to take part in their social climbing plans. I don't fit into my own family anymore. And when I try to make them understand, words start flying around the room that simply can't be taken back. And then I'm full of regret and sadness, and I start doubting my own walk of faith. What's wrong with me?

Like Becca, haven't we all, if we are honest, felt the same way after a conversation has gone wrong? I know I have, more times than I care to recall. We go into a situation prayerful, hopeful, with wonderful expectations. Then, we suddenly find ourselves in the middle of a difficult, painful, and sometimes anger-driven conversation—with the people we love.

For us as believers, we are to keep our eyes on our blessed hope, Jesus Christ, and we eagerly await his return, knowing that as we wait, we are called to *occupy*. What does this mean? In short, it means to be simultaneously awaiting his return, while occupying our world, trying to do good, shed light, serve in love, and speak with compassionate understanding. But all that requires dying to ourselves, every single day. It can also mean dying to our expectations.

Like Becca, we hope that when we share our faith, our hope, and our love for Jesus, the responses we receive will be positive and receptive. But too often, it's just the opposite.

As Becca discovered with each life choice she made that fell in opposition to her parents' plans for her, the divide between them only broadened. Although she did her best to bridge that divide, she soon discovered that her most perfectly planned and prepared conversations frequently ended in anger erupting all around. For her part, she tried to stay calm even when her parents belittled her faith and her life choices. Instead, she prayed that her parents would be persuaded by her self-controlled, upright, and godly life. She hoped they would see that her love for Jesus made her a better, more unselfish and loving daughter. But all they saw was a stranger in their midst, and it frightened them.

So how do we keep on fighting the good fight, trying to love those close to us (family, friends, colleagues, or neighbors) when they don't want any part of Jesus? We can only do as Elyse Fitzpatrick suggests: "You can rest, and in that rest you will find a sweetness growing in your soul that will delight and nourish those around you." We find our rest in Jesus. We surrender our control of trying to convince our loved ones of our faith. We do good to them and for them. When we fail, we ask for forgiveness from God and our loved ones. We begin anew each day, fully aware of and grateful for Jesus' ever-present love, grace, and strength to rest in him—not in our perfect presentation of him.

 Take-away Action Thought

When I find myself discouraged and disgruntled because of a conversation in which I found myself misunderstood and rejected, I will rest in Jesus. I will take myself to a quiet place and thank him for forgiving me, for loving me, for continuing to use me despite my weaknesses and failings. I will find my rest in him and rejoice.

My Heart's Cry to You, O Lord

Father, I want my family and friends to know your love and your forgiveness. I understand what a stretch it is for them to accept my decision to be a Christ follower and to make Jesus Lord of all. It truly does upset all of their plans, ideas, and dreams for me. Yet how can I not share with them the good news of the gospel? I feel compelled to share my faith with those I love. Please help me to be sensitive, wise, and tender with them. Help me to place myself in their position and have compassion for them. Lord, I need your help with the words I choose to say or not to say. Give me the grace I need to live out my faith in a worthy way before them, without even speaking a word. Amen.

Giving Thanks for My Perfectly Imperfect Life

1. This week, I will spend time each day in prayer for those family and friends who do not share my faith in Jesus. I will write down specific verses of promise and pray these promises back to God as I intercede for each of them.

2. I will write down in my journal the name of each person with whom I need to share my faith in Jesus, and I'll commit to memory several verses in which the gospel is made clear. Before I meet with my loved ones, I'll enlist the prayer support of my believing friends.

3. Before the month is over, I want to demonstrate my love for my family and friends by doing good for them and to them. I'll write down specific acts of service that bless and encourage each of these loved ones. Day by day, I'll commit to serving every one of these individuals in ways that spell love to them. I'll love them without saying a word.

Chapter 16

Perfectly Imperfect—Our Holiness

With minds that are alert and fully sober, set your hope
on the grace to be brought to you when Jesus Christ is
revealed at his coming. As obedient children, do not conform
to the evil desires you had when you lived in ignorance.
But just as he who called you is holy, so be holy in all
you do; for it is written: "Be holy, because I am holy."

1 Peter 1:13–16

*Personal holiness is an effect of redemption, not
the cause of it. If we place our faith in human
goodness we will go under when testing comes.*
Oswald Chambers

J illian sat on her bed with her head hung low as she
scrolled through her social media accounts one after another. Before she realized it, she had been scrolling and
swiping for over an hour. *What a waste of time*, she thought as
she turned her phone to silent mode and then flipped it over.
*Mom's right. The more time I spend online, the worse I feel. I
can't stand to see what my friends are posting with all those
likes and comments. It makes me feel sick inside. None of what*

they are sharing is true. Not really. Thinking about her school friends who constantly posted their pictures, updates, and live videos, she found herself comparing her own life with their supposedly perfect online profiles. Except that Jillian knew better. She had been present at much of what they talked about, and she knew that what really happened was considerably different from what they said online.

But am I any better? Jillian asked herself honestly. *Sure, I don't exaggerate or lie about what's really going on in my life. But I'm guilty of comparing myself with others and then judging them. I'm allowing what others say and do (and post) to affect me emotionally. How crazy is that?*

She then recalled the conversation she had with her mom when they were eating lunch at her favorite pizza place that past weekend. *I was so busy looking at my phone I didn't pay much attention to what Mom was saying until she covered it with a napkin. That got my attention. Then Mom began telling me about an article she read about how people who are constantly online feel discouraged, discontent, and even depressed. I get that!*

Her mother then told her that we all have to constantly fight against comparing ourselves to other people, and that the Bible says that those who compare themselves with others are fools. Then she said something Jillian just couldn't get out of her head: The answer to feeling downhearted and discouraged can be found by pursuing holiness. She didn't even know what that meant. How could pursuing holiness make her feel better on the inside?

Her mom explained that when we read the Bible and obey God's commands, we are becoming holy. It's sort of like a math formula, only spiritual. When we trust God and obey what we read in the Bible, we start to change on the inside and we begin to feel different too. *If I don't want to feel so discouraged or dis-*

content, I need to limit my time online, Jillian realized. *I need to be thankful for what God has given me and how he has made me, and pray for others to find that same love for themselves. I need to spend more time in God's presence alone, and stop trying to make my life look wonderful on the outside to impress others.*

Although the pursuit of holiness can be downright confusing, pursue it we must. Let's begin at the beginning. First of all, as Christ followers we need to understand, as Oswald Chambers aptly described it, that "personal holiness is an effect of redemption, not the cause of it. If we place our faith in human goodness we will go under when testing comes." Personal holiness cannot be humanly earned, engineered, bought, or produced. Holiness is a God-given, supernatural gift—and something we should pursue our entire lives.

Pursuing holiness can, and often does, eliminate a lot of emotional baggage. This is because we place our focus on God rather than on people (and their inferior definitions of happiness, fulfillment, and success). As we put our efforts into knowing God, reading his word, meditating on his promises, and praying without ceasing, our minds are gloriously renewed with eternal truth. We begin to think differently. We start to see life through a spiritual lens. We change from the inside out, and often our emotions shift and lift in direct comparison to the personal effort (fueled supernaturally by the Holy Spirit within us) we expend to pursue holiness.

True, holiness is a supernatural product born of being redeemed by God. But as in so many areas of our lives, there's God's part (redemption) and our part (pursuit of holiness). We must choose how to spend our time. We must decide who we will look to for our standard of conduct (God or people). We must put into place those daily habits and disciplines that will bring good into our lives and bring glory to God. Most definitely, personal holiness will never be a perfect endeavor this side of heaven. But pursue it we must.

Take-away Action Thought

I will not allow the world's inferior definitions of happiness, fulfillment, and success to derail my personal pursuit of holiness. Although I realize it will never be a perfect pursuit, because I am human and I will fail, pursue it I will and by God's enabling grace, I will never stop.

My Heart's Cry to You, O Lord

Father, help me to stay focused on what is most important in this life. I often get sidetracked and distracted by everything that is happening all around me. Online. Offline. In my mind. By my emotions. I find it so difficult to take a deep breath and pause, to set aside precious alone time reading the Bible, praying, and meditating on all your wonderful promises. Help me to keep pursuing personal holiness, despite my failings, distractions, and setbacks. I know that your supernatural work in my heart and soul will continue until I see you face-to-face. Until then, help me to seek you first, even though I know my pursuit will be imperfect at best. Amen.

Giving Thanks for My Perfectly Imperfect Life

1. Today, I will spend time alone with the Lord and prayerfully ask him to reveal to me any areas of my life that are hindering my pursuit of personal holiness. I will wait on the Lord to show me how my daily habits may be affecting me emotionally and how certain people may be distracting me from pursuing holiness. I will wait on God to show me the next step.

2. I will reorder my day accordingly to place pursuing God and holiness at the top of my priorities. I'll schedule in time every day on my calendar to ensure I am honoring the Lord by reading his word, praying, and meditating on his promises.

3. Because I understand that accountability is a safeguard to growth, I will ask a few good friends to check in with me every few days and ask me how my pursuit of holiness is unfolding. I'll commit to being honest with them and will ask them to do the same with me. I'm not interested in pursuing perfection or legalism; I want to pursue holiness, even when the path is fraught with mistakes, failings, and weakness.

Chapter 17

Perfectly Imperfect—Our Regrets

Godly sorrow brings repentance that leads to salvation and leaves no regret, but worldly sorrow brings death.
2 Corinthians 7:10

What I had to do was to decide if I would trust Him, even when my heart ached. I realized anew that, just as we must learn to obey God one choice at a time, we must also learn to trust God one circumstance at a time. Trusting God is not a matter of my feelings but of my will. I never feel like trusting God when adversity strikes, but I can choose to do so even when I don't feel like it. That act of the will, though, must be based on belief, and belief must be based on truth.
Jerry Bridges

Too frazzled to cook, Meg rushed out to pick up dinner from a nearby Italian café for her granddaughters. She'd have just enough time to pop the lasagna in the oven to keep it warm, toss the salad, and cut up some fruit before Brittany arrived with the girls.

By the time everything was ready, her oldest daughter arrived with the three girls. "I'm going to be late, Mom," Brittany said in a hurry as she headed back to the car. "I'll text you when I'm on my way. Thanks!" Then she was off.

Meg actually felt relieved that Brittany had to dash off to see Kim. As the girls sat quietly doing some homework before dinner, Meg found herself wondering at God's providential care in arranging this evening—and how she was sure it was all for a purpose larger than she could imagine.

As she puttered around the kitchen with last-minute dinner preparation, she realized how many regrets she had. She looked at her darling little granddaughters, wishing her daughter could talk kinder to them, and not be so impatient and irritated—as Meg herself had been to her own children. It made her heart sink every time she heard her voice, her words, coming out of her daughter's mouth.

She knew she wasn't always the mother she should have been to her children. But now, she felt like she was watching a rerun of her own life being lived out right in front of her with her grandchildren. *Help us, Lord*, she prayed silently. *Help me to move past all my mistakes and failings. Help my daughter to look to you for the help she needs in raising her girls in a way that honors you. I know you want so much more for Brittany. You wanted more for me, but I was too stubborn to listen until it was almost too late.*

Then she realized that today—right now—could be the start of something new. She suddenly felt that something was taking place that she never dreamed could or would happen. She knew that it was God who had orchestrated that chance meeting between Brittany and Meg's best friend, Kim, at the orchard last week. *Only you could have given my dear friend Kim just the right words of loving concern to say to my world-weary daughter in a way that she would listen and hear.*

Only you know how much hope I feel in my heart of hearts when I think about Kim having the opportunity to speak life into

Brittany's life . . . and Brittany receiving it. Oh, Lord, she prayed again. *Please help my friend to be sensitive to the Holy Spirit's leading as she enters into the difficult waters of my daughter's life, her marriage, and her parenting. Help my daughter to have a soft heart, listening ears, and a tenderness toward you. Thank you, Father, for using godly sorrow to bring us to repentance and salvation.*

"Godly sorrow brings repentance that leads to salvation and leaves no regret, but worldly sorrow brings death." Doesn't this verse from 2 Corinthians 7:10 speak to the whole area of regrets perfectly? Consider this: the type of sorrow that God uses to bring us to repentance does us good. God reveals to our stubborn, sinful hearts how far we are from his standard of righteousness. When we listen to the Holy Spirit's gentle tugging, and we say yes to the forgiveness offered through Christ's perfect sacrifice on the cross, we begin life anew. We are born again. The old has gone. The new has come. Praise be to God!

Godly sorrow is the direct opposite of that hopeless, worldly sorrow that only brings death. Our hearts break for those we know and love who won't receive Christ's perfect gift of salvation through grace and forgiveness for our sins. I was so drawn to Meg and Brittany's story, because in part I've lived it. Like every parent I know, I don't have to reflect too far back in my own years of parenting to remember all the failures and mistakes I made.

Like Meg and Brittany, I can still remember impatiently lashing out at my children, irritated because I felt they didn't obey me quickly enough. On the outside, desiring my children to immediately obey is a good thing. But on the inside of my imperfect perfectionist heart, I knew I was frustrated because I just wanted the day to be more efficient, smoother. And if my children would just listen and obey, then my parenting job would be much easier.

How regretful I feel whenever I hear my own children respond to their children as I did in my not so patient moments. How grateful I am today when others, like Kim, come alongside my adult children to help encourage, guide, and bless them with parenting wisdom. How fitting then, especially for all of us perfectionists, to do as Jerry Bridges suggests in the wake of our own personal failings that affect others negatively: "What I had to do was to decide if I would trust Him, even when my heart ached."

 ## Take-away Action Thought

When I start to feel the regret of past mistakes that have negatively impacted those I love, I will turn my heart toward Jesus and begin thanking him for always making up the difference in my lack of patience and perspective with his grace, strength, and power. I will turn my sorrow into godly joy and be thankful for Jesus' perfect sacrifice for me.

My Heart's Cry to You, O Lord

Father, today I was painfully reminded of how in the past I have failed those I love. I am keenly aware of my impatience, my irritation, and my frustration that used to seep out of my heart and into my words. Please, Lord, help me to move past these painful memories and keep my focus on you alone. I have already asked for forgiveness from you and from those I hurt with my sinful words and actions. But sometimes, when I see how my mistakes impacted my family and they are now repeating my poor example, it pains me so deeply. I know, however, that godly sorrow brings salvation and no regret. Thank you for the perfect gift of salvation through Jesus' sacrifice. Amen.

Giving Thanks for My Perfectly Imperfect Life

1. I will trust God even when my heart aches. This week, I will focus on praying through all my old regrets and giving them the space I need to work through them. I'll spend time each day talking to the Lord about any areas that fill my heart with pain when I am reminded of the past. Then I will thank the Lord for the godly sorrow that brought me to salvation.

2. I will obey God one choice at a time. Day by day, I will keep my heart and mind renewed by reading God's word every morning and every evening. I will prayerfully reflect on my day and ask the Lord to help me be sensitive to the Holy Spirit's leading when I make choices. Then I will thank the Lord for the godly sorrow that brought me to salvation.

3. I will trust God, one circumstance at a time. Each day, I will begin my time with God by thanking him in advance for the strength, peace, and grace I will need to meet all my responsibilities in a way that honors him. I will memorize a verse of my choosing on trusting God and keep it with me to refer to as needed. Then, once again, I will thank the Lord for the godly sorrow that brought me to salvation.

 Chapter 18

Perfectly Imperfect—Our Contentment

I know what it is to be in need, and I know what it
is to have plenty. I have learned the secret of being
content in any and every situation, whether well fed
or hungry, whether living in plenty or in want. I can
do all this through him who gives me strength.

Philippians 4:12–13

*At all times, in all circumstances, Christ is able and willing
to provide the strength we need to be content. Contentment
occurs when Christ's strength is infused into my weak body,
soul, and spirit. To infuse means to pour, fill, soak, or extract.
Every morning when I dip my herbal tea bag into boiling
water, I witness infusion. How does God enable us to be
content? He infuses contentment into us through His Word.
As it seeps into our minds, it transforms us. Just as a cup of
tea gets stronger when we give it time to steep, so we become
more content when we spend time in God's Word and allow
it to seep into our lives, transforming us to be like Him.*

Linda Dillow

Renee kept looking at her text messages, waiting anxiously for word of Carly's surgery results from Renee's son-in-law, Joel. Renee tried to push from her thoughts the life-threatening outcome from Carly's surgery two years earlier. It had been a simple, low-risk procedure that turned into a nightmarish time in ICU, as they waited for ten days to see if she would survive. After the initial crisis was over, Carly's healing took much longer than the surgeon had expected for a healthy twenty-six-year-old. But eventually, Carly's body healed, and she was able to go back to college and her part-time job as a receptionist.

Renee didn't realize, however, that her daughter had been in pain every single day for months after her surgeon cleared her to return to school and work. Renee didn't learn of Carly's health struggles until the night that Joel called her. Distressed, he begged her to try to get Carly to have further tests. Joel knew something was still wrong with her, but Carly was now surgery shy after her first traumatic outcome. Of course, Renee called her, getting her to agree that something needed to be done about her incessant pain. Fast-forward to eight weeks and a series of exams and medical tests later, when Carly was being wheeled into the operating room for exploratory surgery.

Although Renee wanted to fly out to be there, she was limited in money and time. She had to settle for driving out after the surgery, but then she could stay with Carly and Joel while Carly recovered at home. Renee thought the plan (imperfect at best) was the wisest given their (imperfect at best) circumstances. But now that her beloved daughter was actually in surgery, she began having serious doubts about the wisdom of that decision. *Lord*, she prayed, *help me to calm down inside. Help me to stay focused on you and not give way to my emotions and fear.*

You are in control of this situation. You love my Carly more than I ever will, for yours is a perfect love. Help guide my prayers and give me the grace to be content to be here where I can intercede on her behalf. Amen.

Some say it's much harder and far more draining to be the loved one sitting in a waiting room (or as in Renee's case, states away), intently listening for the surgeon's footfall, than it is to be the patient in the operating room. I've been in both situations, and I say they are equally challenging. This is why I love Paul's declaration that no matter what the circumstance, we can say along with him,

> I have learned the secret of being content in any and every situation, whether well fed or hungry, whether living in plenty or in want. I can do all this through him who gives me strength.

I liken these words "I can do all this" to mean that God will infuse me with the strength I need to do what is needful in that moment. And that is perfect within an imperfect situation.

In Renee's "moment," she needed to be infused with the knowledge of who God is and how much he loves her daughter. Renee was needful of grace, peace, wisdom, and contentment. But how challenging it is when we find ourselves agreeing to those imperfect solutions to those imperfect circumstances. We may say yes, but in our heart of hearts we struggle to accept the situation.

So how do we learn to be content in those perfectly imperfect scenarios, when every ounce of our beings wants to be somewhere else? As Paul stated, he learned through practice and experience, through hard times and good times, through seasons of want and seasons of plenty, that he could be content through the strength God provided. Paul exhorts us to follow his example and learn to be content by relying on the strength God provides for us today. How do we activate this strength, this contentment? Linda Dillow says it best:

> Just as a cup of tea gets stronger when we give it time to steep, so we become more content when we spend time in God's Word and allow it to seep into our lives, transforming us to be like Him.

 Take-away Action Thought

When I am struggling to be content in my present circumstances, I will infuse myself more deeply into God's word and allow his truth to seep into every area of my mind. I will prayerfully meditate on his word, so that God's powerful promises can transform me to be like him.

My Heart's Cry to You, O Lord

Father, on those ordinary days of life when no crisis or tragedy is assaulting me or those I love, it's easy to feel content. But when the battle is against me and I'm forced to fight for peace of mind, for faith-fueled thoughts, and for contentment in the middle of the storm, I discover who I really am. Help me to be mindful that I must spend time every single day in your word and with you in prayer, so that I am equipped for those assaults. Clothe me with your divine wisdom and understanding, so that I will think biblically and not fall into a state of doubt or discontent. Help me to honor you by being thankful and content no matter what the circumstance, because I know you love me with a love that is nothing less than perfect. Amen.

Giving Thanks for My Perfectly Imperfect Life

1. Today, I will sit down with a cup of tea and my Bible and journal. I will watch as my tea bag infuses the water with its flavor and aroma. As I observe this visual transformation, I will select several verses that speak of contentment and write them in my journal. I'll meditate on each verse's meaning and how their promises can strengthen and comfort me in times of trouble by infusing me with eternal truth.

2. This week, I'll make note of any upcoming events or personally challenging circumstances where I anticipate struggling to be content. I will honestly pray about each of these instances and ask the Lord to help me to be truly content before, during, and after each one. I will commit to memory this verse from Philippians 4:12–13: "I can do all this through him who gives me strength."

3. At the end of the week, I will spend some quiet moments reviewing both my attitude and my actions from the past seven days. I'll reflect on my contentment levels given each challenging circumstance, and ask myself how meditating on Bible verses equipped me to be content with my perfectly imperfect situations.

 # Chapter 19

Perfectly Imperfect—Our Sorrow

The LORD is gracious and righteous;
    our God is full of compassion.
The LORD protects the unwary;
    when I was brought low, he saved me.
Return to your rest, my soul,
    for the LORD has been good to you.
For you, LORD, have delivered me from death,
    my eyes from tears,
    my feet from stumbling,
that I may walk before the LORD
    in the land of the living.

Psalm 116:5–9

I have trusted thee and thou hast not betrayed my trust;
waited for thee, and not waited in vain.
Thou wilt come to raise my body from the dust,
and re-unite it to my soul,
by a wonderful work of infinite power and love,
greater than that which bounds the oceans' waters,
ebbs and flows the tides,
keeps the stars in their courses,
and gives life to all creatures. . . .

*I triumph now in thy promises as I shall do
in their performance.*

A Puritan Prayer

R osa was just finishing up her latest twelve-month watercolor floral calendar for an upcoming art show, and she was excited to share her final presentation with her fellow artists. She routinely created handmade artwork, paintings, greeting cards, and calendars that sold out fast every year. Her buyers frequently commented that the flowers in her paintings seemed real enough to smell. This made her happy, because that was her intent: to recreate beauty, color, and life to inspire folks, especially during long dormant winter seasons. Today, she planned to hand deliver one of her calendars to a friend from her church, Stacy, who had been on her mind.

Rosa knew Stacy quite well, but they hadn't connected in months and something inside nudged her to visit Stacy. So today, Rosa set aside an hour to drive over to Stacy's home after she left her studio. Carefully wrapping up her floral calendar in multicolored tissue paper, Rosa sealed the gift with an embossed label of her own design that read, *The Lord is gracious and righteous; our God is full of compassion.*

While on her way, Rosa felt a sudden urge to pray for her friend, so she did. *Lord,* she prayed silently. *I'm not sure why Stacy has been on my mind so much lately and I don't know what's going on in her life right now, but I feel compelled to keep praying for her. Please help me to bring her encouragement.*

When she arrived, she rang Stacy's doorbell, explaining that God had been putting her on her mind. Stacy offered Rosa some iced tea that Rosa happily accepted. Sipping their drinks at the kitchen table, Rosa looked up and noticed Stacy's three-year-old yellowed wall calendar. When Rosa asked Stacy why it was still there, Stacy paused and then said, "I haven't touched it since Monica died. I just can't part with it. It's still on the same page as when she passed away. I suppose I just don't have the heart to take it down."

Rosa took her hand and said, "Oh, I'm so sorry." She sat for a minute and then said, "I wonder if I have something here that might help." Handing Stacy her package, Rosa watched and waited. She didn't know if her gift would be a blessing or add more pain to her friend's sorrowing heart. But Rosa knew she had to try and help relieve even a small portion of that broken heart.

"Oh . . . it's beautiful," Stacy whispered through tears. "You made this? For me? I don't know what to say . . . but I think I know what I need to do." She took down the old calendar and replaced it with this beautiful new one. "Hope," she said, admiring it. "This calendar looks and feels like hope. Thank you. Thank you so much."

With tears welling in her own eyes, Rosa hugged her friend tightly—thankful she hadn't shushed that still small voice from the Lord. So very thankful.

When I heard this story, I wept. I thought about the silent private pain Stacy was enduring long after her daughter had died. I reflected on how that faded, outdated calendar represented her state of mind and emotions. Stacy was grief-stricken, feeling hopeless, feeling purposeless. We can imagine her pain and how her heart will always sorrow for her daughter until heaven's grand reunion. When I considered what God had done by prompting Rosa to visit her friend and bring the perfect gift to brighten Stacy's heart and mind, I felt overcome by awe and gratitude.

When we are in the midst of life's sorrows (and there are many), I wonder if we grasp the healing power of the Psalms. If there's one book in the Bible that overflows with human emotion, it's the Psalms. No matter what we're feeling, there's a psalm to help us unpack those intense emotions.

The portion of Psalm 116 above shares the greatest contrasts of all: life and death. It also helps us to cling all the more tightly to God and his eternal promises in the middle of our darkest seasons, by reminding us of this truth: "The Lord is gracious and righteous; our God is full of compassion." By the end of this section, the psalmist is able to say that God has drawn close and mended his heart so that his tears have dried, and he has received rest and protection, walking once again among the land of the living. Wow! What a transformation—one that awaits me and you when we turn to God in the midst of our sorrows and wait for him. But let's not forget that there is no perfect formula for sorrow or grief. It's messy. It's imperfect. It's part of our human experience. And yet God, in the midst of all its imperfection and messiness, makes a way out of the darkness and into his marvelous light.

 Take-away Action Thought

I will grieve, but I refuse to grieve endlessly. Instead, I will remember God's graciousness, righteousness, and compassion. I will wait for the Lord to minister his healing, his rest, his protection, and his strength to me.

My Heart's Cry to You, O Lord

Father, my heart is full of sorrow, and I cannot imagine when or how I will be able to stop grieving this loss. I understand that I'll never get over this pain, but that I'll learn to live with it. Please draw near to me now and help me to cry my tears and then rest quietly until I've regained my strength. As I wait on you to begin healing my broken heart, I will call to mind your graciousness, your righteousness, and your compassion. I'll begin thanking you for your nearness to me in this time of sorrow. And I'll keep looking for you every hour of every day. Amen.

Giving Thanks for My Perfectly Imperfect Life

1. "I triumph now in thy promises as I shall do in their performance." I will spend time reflecting on specific moments when God helped me pass through seasons of sorrow. I'll write out verses that pair up with his past faithfulness to me. Then I will reflect upon how gracious, righteous, and compassionate God has been with me.

2. "I triumph now in thy promises as I shall do in their performance." This week, I will spend time reflecting on any sorrows I'm in the midst of right now. I'll search out several verses that will help comfort me in this season of grieving. Then, I'll say these verses out loud and thank the Lord for his faithfulness to answered prayer even before the answer comes.

3. "I triumph now in thy promises as I shall do in their performance." At the end of the week, I'll prayerfully ask the Lord to reveal to my mind any specific sorrows I have about the unknown future. Do I have fears that make me sorrowful? Am I sad when I think about the coming days, because of the losses I've already experienced? I'll then find and write out a few verses to strengthen my heart and mind for tomorrow.

 # Chapter 20

Perfectly Imperfect—Our Lord's Timing

> How precious to me are your thoughts, God!
>> How vast is the sum of them!
> Were I to count them,
>> they would outnumber the grains of the sand. . . .
>
> Search me, God, and know my heart;
>> test me and know my anxious thoughts.
> See if there is any offensive way in me,
>> and lead me in the way everlasting.
>
> Psalm 139:17–18, 23–24

Gospel humility is not needing to think about myself. Not needing to connect things with myself. True gospel humility means not connecting every experience, every conversation, with myself. In fact, I stop thinking about myself. The freedom of self-forgetfulness. The blessed rest that only self-forgetfulness brings.

Tim Keller

B rielle sat across from her husband, Jack, and listened intently as he discussed his thoughts about retiring early from his almost forty-year-teaching career at the nearby Christian high school. Although everything inside of her started to tense up, she tried not to show it. Years earlier, they had made plans that included him working until age sixty-five. Jack was now sixty-two. Brielle understood, in part, her spouse's reasons for wanting to retire three years sooner than planned. But being the planning ultra-perfectionist that she was, she was having a difficult time wrapping her mind around this sudden change of their long-term goals.

Brielle sighed to herself and thought, *If Jack retires now, then our healthcare plans just went out the window—along with that higher retirement check if he waited to retire at age sixty-five. Plus, what will Jack do every day with his time? I'm still working from home and don't plan to stop anytime soon. Having Jack here day in and day out will most certainly affect my ability to work effectively from my home office.* Brielle tore her mind away from all the what-ifs and how-tos and why-nots and tried to concentrate again on Jack's explanations.

Finally, she interrupted her husband and said, "Jack, I don't know if it's the wisest decision—you retiring this year. Remember all of our plans? We talked about your monthly retirement check and our healthcare options. If you leave at the end of this school year, all that changes. We really need to pray and think about this before making a final decision. I'm not convinced this is the right time."

Jack nodded his head slowly, considering her words. "I understand your concerns, Brielle. I've considered every one of them, but I have prayed about this decision and I've come up with a good alternative plan for us. With my health issues, teaching is getting harder and harder. I want to switch gears and devote more time to you, our kids, and our grandchildren. And I want to spend more time each week with my men's group prison ministry. I won't do anything of course without your agreement, but I do ask that you prayerfully consider this change of plans."

It was then Brielle's turn to nod her head slowly as she considered Jack's words, but she couldn't help wanting to fight against any kind of change—especially one like this that was so important, one that disrupted her perfectly designed no-fail plan! She took a deep breath and prayed silently: *Right now, Lord, I need you to help me focus on the biblical truth that you will always supply what we need. You have promised to care for us every day of our lives. With your help, I can accept these changes with good grace and a robust faith. I admit that I worry about getting my needs met because of my fear of not being in control. If this timing is best for Jack, then help me to see it and embrace it. Help me, Lord, to place all of my trust in you alone today and for all our tomorrows. Amen.*

Oh, the inner angst and struggle we endure when our will and timing collide with another's will and timing—not to mention God's will and timing. The struggle is real. It is especially painful for the perfectionist who, like Brielle, plans with detail and a determination to calculate risk factors and eliminate them one by one. But, oh, the freedom Tim Keller talks about when believers (even those stubborn perfectionists like me!) embrace gospel humility and discover "the freedom of self-forgetfulness. The blessed rest that only self-forgetfulness brings." What a beautiful picture this "self-forgetfulness" brings to mind. No matter what the circumstance, we need to remember that God is in control, God can be trusted, and God has the means to supply everything we will ever need.

This word, *self-forgetfulness*, is so powerful and freeing to perfectionists in particular, because we admittedly tend to expend far too much mental energy trying to maneuver, massage, and manipulate our circumstances to ensure the very best outcomes. Don't we? There is indeed a blessed freedom that can be ours when we lift our focus off of our circumstances and onto God. As Keller writes, "True gospel humility means not connecting every experience, every conversation, with myself. In fact, I stop thinking about myself. The freedom of self-forgetfulness. The blessed rest that only self-forgetfulness brings." I pray we can learn to forget about ourselves more and more with each passing day, so we can begin to enjoy the blessed gift of freedom that self-forgetfulness brings.

 Take-away Action Thought

When unexpected changes in plans or timing come my way, I will resist the temptation to become anxious. I will intentionally practice self-forgetfulness, placing my focus on God and on serving others and meeting their needs.

My Heart's Cry to You, O Lord

Father, I feel off-kilter and shaken up inside, because all of my carefully laid plans are being cast aside. Although I'm not sure this is the best way or the ideal time to make these changes, I'm trying not to panic. Please remind me that you have promised to meet my every need. Don't let me forget that you are always mindful of me and of whatever is going on in my life. Help me to honor you, Lord, by trusting you above all. I want to respond with good grace when changes in timing come my way. But it isn't easy. You know how I try to make perfect plans for every eventuality. Lord, this is not living by faith, nor is it the path to inner freedom. Help me keep my eyes on you during these changes so I can stay calm and enjoy the peace you bring that surpasses all understanding. Amen.

Giving Thanks for My Perfectly Imperfect Life

1. This week, I will set aside time to reflect on this passage in Psalm 139 that tells me how much God thinks about me: more than the grains of sand! In other words, God thinks about me beyond count. I will commit verses 17 and 18 to memory: "How precious to me are your thoughts, God! How vast is the sum of them! Were I to count them, they would outnumber the grains of the sand."

2. I will also reflect on verses 23 and 24, prayerfully asking the Lord to reveal to me any areas in which I'm fearful and struggling to trust him. "Search me, God, and know my heart; test me and know my anxious thoughts. See if there is any offensive way in me, and lead me in the way everlasting."

3. I'll write down specific ways I can practice self-forgetfulness this week. I will consider my family, my friends, and my work associates and complete a list of daily ways I can place my focus on meeting their needs. Through this exercise, I will also pray for that inner freedom that comes when I intentionally focus on God and on others.

 Chapter 21

Perfectly Imperfect—Our Shame

In all their distress he too was distressed,
    and the angel of his presence saved them.
In his love and mercy he redeemed them;
    he lifted them up and carried them
    all the days of old.

Isaiah 63:9

And in all your suffering, He suffers. He is with you, right in the midst of it. Helping you. Loving you. Hurting with you. Driving you back to Him, drawing you closer in, making you more dependent upon His grace and power. As you get to know and trust His heart, you will be able to face the cross—the way Christ faced it from the haunting shadows of Gethsemane—and still say, even through your tears, "Not my will, but Yours be done."

Nancy Leigh DeMoss

Erica felt ashamed of her feelings. She knew that her parents loved her, but they seemed aloof and even shut off emotionally. While Erica was gregarious and a real people lover, her parents were reserved to the point of being repressive and never expressed their emotions. Nor were they comfortable when Erica expressed hers. They didn't seem to understand Erica's outgoing personality or her love for big expressions of affection.

As Erica grew older, she wondered why she was so very different from her mother and father. That is, until her sixteenth birthday, when they told her that they had adopted her as a baby. *Happy Birthday to me*, Erica thought sarcastically. Erica's adoptive parents had waited until now to disclose this life-altering news, because they believed that it would have been too painful for her to process at a younger age. But even at sixteen, this news was still completely life changing.

She didn't take long before approaching her adoptive parents to ask them to help her locate her birth parents. In response, they asked her to wait until she turned eighteen. She agreed to honor their wishes, but those two long years of wondering and waiting were hard on all of them. Erica now understood why she was so different from her parents in personality, but that knowledge only added to her pain and shame. She also struggled against a growing resentment toward her adoptive parents for keeping the truth from her for so long. She reasoned, true or not, that if she had grown up knowing she was adopted, she wouldn't be going through such a crisis now.

Erica often spent her quiet moments thinking—and overthinking—about what her life may have been like if her birth parents had not given her up. This then led to the question: Why did they give her up for adoption? She imagined any number of likely and unlikely scenarios and reasons why she went into the foster care system as an infant. If her adoptive parents knew the truth, however, they weren't sharing it.

She swung from feeling angry to feeling ashamed, because she knew her adoptive mother and father loved her. They did. *So why am I so upset?* Erica thought sadly. *Why do I feel betrayed? I should be grateful. I am grateful. I just don't understand why this hurts so much. Is it wrong for me to want to know who my birth parents are? When I ask my parents about them, I can see how much it hurts them and then I feel ashamed again. I almost wish my parents had never told me the truth. It hurts too much!*

Erica's story is yet another example of our perfectly imperfect lives where the decisions of others impact us greatly and often at great cost, to us and to them. Reading her story and understanding her pain and shame for feeling angry and resentful toward her adoptive parents makes my heart ache. We do feel pain, and then frequently we feel shame for feeling pain. We tell ourselves (rightly) that we have so much to be thankful for. While we may understand intellectually that our pain is legitimate, our emotions can easily swing in the opposite direction so that we feel shame for feeling hurt. Somehow we have to break this vicious cycle.

God has a better path for us to traverse through our heartaches and pain and shame. It is a perfectly imperfect path to be sure, but one that will bring inner healing, forgiveness, and restoration. One of the most vital truths we as Christians need to know and internalize is that God hurts right along with us. Our heavenly Father is not like Erica's adoptive parents, who were emotionally distant. Never.

> And in all your suffering, He suffers. He is with you, right in the midst of it. Helping you. Loving you. Hurting with you. Driving you back to Him, drawing you closer in, making you more dependent upon His grace and power.

I love how DeMoss points us directly back to the heart of God, encouraging us to put our complete trust in the One who created us. None of us want to be in a place where pain, shame, and blame take front and center in our hearts and minds. But we always have a choice, don't we? We can dig in our heels and let everyone know how much their actions hurt us. We can refuse to offer forgiveness to those we believe wounded us. Or we can press closer into Jesus' love and allow him to start the process of healing our hearts, apart from the imperfect love that others show us.

When we choose Jesus, only then can we truly say "Thy will be done" and mean it. When we accept Jesus' love toward us, our pain and shame can be transformed into healing and hope and the peace that defies human understanding.

 ## Take-away Action Thought

When I am feeling pain and shame, I will go to God and be honest with all my feelings. I will not suppress them or reject them, but I will ask the Lord to help me work through them.

My Heart's Cry to You, O Lord

Father, here I am, feeling all these painful emotions again over circumstances I cannot change. I want to come to you with a heart overflowing with gratitude, not one immersed in shame and resentment. Please help me to work through my emotions and find comfort and security as your beloved child. I know that I will never fully grasp all the "whys" in this life. But I want your will to be done even when, especially when, I don't understand. I trust your love for me, Jesus. I know you hurt when I hurt; you suffer when I suffer. You want me to look to you for peace, grace, and comfort. Help me to cast off this guilt and shame and turn toward the light I need to carry on. Amen.

Giving Thanks for My Perfectly Imperfect Life

1. My perfectly imperfect emotions. When my emotions start to swing wildly from one end of the spectrum to the other, I will take a deep breath and then exhale. And repeat. I will calm myself down physically, as I ask the Lord to help me regain my inner peace. I won't do it perfectly, but I will make this practice a habit until I instinctively learn to turn to God for the inner peace I need, which will in turn settle my emotions.

2. My perfectly imperfect responses. I will adopt the pray/think/act principle so that I do not overreact in the face of difficult and intense emotions. I will pray about why I'm feeling as I do and think about the reasons. I know my responses won't be perfect, but I will make progress over time by praying/thinking/acting.

3. My perfectly imperfect understanding. When I am embroiled in confusion and feel shame because of my emotional responses, I will turn to Scripture for the truth of God's love for me. I'll search out Scriptures that define Jesus' heart for me, and I will meditate on them even when my personal circumstances don't feel right to me. I will thank God for his care for me, and by faith I will pray, "Thy will be done."

 Chapter 22

Perfectly Imperfect—Our Forgiveness

If we confess our sins, he is faithful and just and will
forgive us our sins and purify us from all unrighteousness.
1 John 1:9

If He has forgiven us, our slate is clean. . . .
Forgiveness is too big a miracle to expect of ourselves.
To rely on it is to wish for something that can never be.
God is your forgiver—your one and only forgiver.
Nancy Leigh DeMoss

Not too long ago, I took part in two radio interviews that focused on my book *Caring for Our Aging Parents*, which describes our family's caregiving journey for two of our elderly relatives. A woman who was being interviewed with me was a dynamic single gal who had taken care of her elderly mother for several years until she had passed away. My story entailed our first caregiving experience for my husband's elderly second cousin and neighbor, who had been an only child, had never married, and had no children. When the host asked us both what was hardest about our caregiving experiences, we both admitted how draining (in every way possible) and time-consuming caregiving can quickly become. With tears in our eyes, we both described those heartbreaking moments when our frazzled and weary emotions didn't match our acts of loving service.

For my part, I remembered how often I would eye our telephone with dread because every call might be our neighbor asking me to come right over (for perhaps the fourth time that morning) or add another task he needed done immediately to my already overburdened schedule (to my mind at least). I felt ashamed at my heart response and asked forgiveness from the Lord each time my attitude took a dark, sinful turn into resentment and/or bitterness. Certainly, those five years of caregiving for our neighbor did deplete Jim and me mentally, emotionally, physically, and even spiritually; but I never regretted our choice to love and serve him as we did.

We need God's forgiveness. We need, at times, others' forgiveness. What I struggle with to this day, however, is forgiving myself when I remember my poor attitude and internal responses during those caregiving years. Being the recovering perfectionist that I am, I admit to seeing life as black and white, right and wrong, do or don't, one extreme or another. These tendencies to view life (and all that makes up my life) with an all-or-nothing mentality does me no good. I believe perfectionists like myself especially struggle when our attitudes, actions, reactions, or words do not line up perfectly with the Bible's commands to love with perfect maturity (see 1 Corinthians 13). I get irritated with myself for falling short, as it pertains to serving others selflessly with no end in sight. This is why I must embrace God's forgiveness alone every time I fall short. And fall short I do, daily. And for that, I'm eternally grateful for this passage of Scripture:

If we confess our sins, he is faithful and just and will forgive us our sins and purify us from all unrighteousness. (1 John 1:9)

The problem with perfectionists is that we're really hard on ourselves and can experience difficulty forgiving ourselves. But when we err and ask for God's forgiveness, we're then placing ourselves at his divine mercy. First John 1:9 promises us that "if we confess our sins, he is faithful and just and will forgive us our sins and purify us from all unrighteousness." God's part is to forgive. My part is to grow ever more thankful for God's forgiveness and to be mindful that my sin (any sin) grieves his heart. And if I know that he has forgiven me, then I am forgiven indeed and I need to remind my perfectionist self of this truth!

Besides forgiving myself, I need to seek others' forgiveness as needed and to begin a work of inner sanctification and change within my heart. Rather than my perfectionist all-or-nothing view of life, I must purpose to keep in step with the Spirit moment by moment. In other words, I must stop being a legalist (in my heart and through my actions), embrace God's good gift of forgiveness, and then mercifully forgive others as God has forgiven me. By not expecting perfection in myself, I am free to more fully love and serve others with the unconditional love that 1 Corinthians 13 depicts.

Take-away Action Thought

When I sin, I will ask for God's forgiveness. When I sin against others, I will seek their forgiveness. I will thank the good Lord for cleansing me from all unrighteousness.

My Heart's Cry to You, O Lord

Father, I cannot count the times when I've justified myself because I wanted to feel better about my sin. Even though I believe that you have forgiven me through Jesus, I somehow still cling onto that guilt. All I need, all I will ever need, is your forgiveness. Please help me to fully understand the depth and breadth of your divine forgiveness and how once I confess my sins to you, you have promised to cleanse me from all unrighteousness. Amen.

Giving Thanks for My Perfectly Imperfect Life

1. God's forgiveness. I will commit 1 John 1:9 to memory: "If we confess our sins, he is faithful and just and will forgive us our sins and purify us from all unrighteousness." Each time I knowingly sin, I will ask for God's forgiveness and then thank him that all I ever need is his pardon.

2. Others' forgiveness. When I have sinned against another person, I will seek them out and ask for their forgiveness. I will make it a priority to ask their forgiveness and begin the process of reconciliation as quickly as I can. I will then thank that person for forgiving me.

3. Living forgiven and made righteous. I will daily spend time before the Lord, asking him to reveal to me any sin I may not be aware of or that needs to be forgiven. I will search out verses that include the word *forgiveness* and write down several to commit to memory.

 Chapter 23

Perfectly Imperfect—Our Expectations

"The LORD bless you
and keep you;
the LORD make his face shine on you
and be gracious to you;
the LORD turn his face toward you
and give you peace."

Numbers 6:24–26

At the very darkest moment of his life, when he was
suffering more than anyone had ever suffered or would
ever suffer again, when he should have been vindicated
by his Father and rescued by angels, the heavens were
brass, and yet he obeyed! Oh, glorious obedience! In
all the days when I'm filled with despair because of my
sin, and when I can't find God if my life depended on it;
when I give up in fear, doubt, guilt, and despair, I have
his righteousness—a righteousness that was lived out for
me, on my behalf, and upon which I can rest. Oh, thank
you, glorious God. Having loved us, he loved us to the end.

Elyse Fitzpatrick

S ophie was sitting next to her cousin, Grace, at the first meeting of a women's nine-month-long in-depth Bible study held at a local church. Sophie had been so excited when Grace invited her to join this weekly study of over two hundred women from the community, but she felt nervous too. She had never been in a study before that warned its members that there would be at least one hour of homework every day, for every week, all year long. Grace had already been attending this systematic study for several years, and she assured her cousin that she would be able to handle it. Sophie, the family's reigning perfectionist, wondered if it was possible for her to do this. *What might take the average person one hour could very well take me three*, Sophie thought. *And I do not have three hours a day to spend doing homework!*

Nevertheless, Grace persisted in her invitations until Sophie accepted. Sitting there among so many women, none of whom Sophie knew, she felt overwhelmed by it all. She could scarcely answer any of the questions before the Bible teacher went to the platform to begin the lesson. After a brief prayer and some opening remarks, the teacher began reading and then dissecting the book of Ephesians verse by verse. She explained the social setting, the history of the people, and the political and religious tensions, all of which mesmerized Sophie. After about forty-five minutes of this lecture, the women broke up into small groups of eight or fewer.

For a single terrifying moment, Sophie wanted to rush out the door when she and Grace were separated during the group discussion. Sophie felt all her old insecurities and inadequacies rise up. *I can't handle this*, she thought to herself, trying not to panic. *I'm not a Bible scholar. I won't know the answers to any of the questions. I will look like a fool. Why did I agree to come? I feel like my brain is going to explode!* Lost within a minefield of warring thoughts and emotions, she felt paralyzed by familiar fears.

123

Then another thought, which seemed to come out of no-where, charged past the rest: *Grow up, Sophie! Put on your big girl pants and find a seat! What's the worst that can happen? So what if you can't answer a question!* Head raised and shoulders braced, Sophie walked determinedly to her seat in the circle and sat down. *Lord, I have no idea what to expect from this dis-cussion*, she silently prayed. *So please help me to relax and get as much out of this part of the study as I just did from the lecture.*

Like so many perfectionists, Sophie feels a compulsion to know what is going to happen at every step of a process, a plan, a party, a meeting, and even a women's Bible study. It's just the way she is wired. In similar style, many perfectionists like Sophie tend to overthink their options. For Sophie, she was honestly afraid that she didn't have the Bible knowledge or the answers to potential questions, which almost paralyzed her from participating. Her self-imposed expectations of per-fection almost ended her part in this dynamic study before it even began. I cannot count the number of times I've listened to people say, "I'm just not comfortable doing that." To which I want to reply, "Neither am I!" But forge ahead we must, because on the other side of our fears blessings await.

Consider how freeing it would be if we did not expect our-selves or others to perform perfectly—how that would change our thoughts, attitudes, and actions. God wants me to know that his love for me is enough for me. Because it is. When I reflect on Jesus' sacrifice on the cross, when he bore the weight of the world's sins upon his shoulders, I wonder how I have the audacity to hold my self-imposed perfectionist expectations (of myself or of a situation) as being worthy of notice.

The deeper I look into the love of God, the less I need to "perform perfectly," because his love and his perfect acceptance of me is all I need. Numbers 6:24–26 makes me light up from the inside out. Why? It reveals, I believe, how Jesus wants us to see him, how he sees us through his love. Read it for yourself and reflect on Jesus' perfect love toward us. Imagine his face turned toward you giving you peace. "The LORD bless you and keep you; the LORD make his face shine on you and be gracious to you; the LORD turn his face toward you and give you peace."

 ## Take-away Action Thought

When I become distracted by self-imposed expectations of myself that hinder me from entering into an unfamiliar situation where God is leading me, I will remember Jesus' perfect sacrifice for me on the cross. I do not have to give way to fear, doubt, guilt, or despair, for I have been made righteous through him.

My Heart's Cry to You, O Lord

Father, I am struggling again with my expectations of both myself and the situations in which I find myself. I've been allowing these thoughts of fear, doubt, guilt, and despair to derail me again. Help me to remember who I am in you, Jesus. I have been made righteous through your sacrifice. I do not have to strive for perfection or impose unrealistic expectations on myself. You want me to turn my face toward you and allow your love to shine fully upon me. Then, and only then, will I have the peace I so desire. Amen.

Giving Thanks for My Perfectly Imperfect Life

1. Perfectly imperfect expectations of myself. I will spend time writing down areas in which I self-impose unrealistic expectations of myself. I'll then pray and ask the Lord to help me transfer my focus away from myself and onto him and his perfect enabling.

2. Perfectly imperfect expectations of situations. This week, I'll reflect on specific experiences that could have been so much more rewarding and fruitful had I not gone into them with unrealistic expectations. I will write down a verse next to each event that reveals the value of the experience, and I will then focus on those blessings and benefits.

3. Perfectly imperfect expectations of God. I will prayerfully ask the Lord to show me if I have wrong thoughts of him, as it pertains to how he created me, how he provides for my needs, or how he loves me. Then I will write down Numbers 6:24–26 and commit it to memory as a visual picture of his tender love for me. "The LORD bless you and keep you; the LORD make his face shine on you and be gracious to you; the LORD turn his face toward you and give you peace."

Chapter 24

Perfectly Imperfect—Our Joy

Yet I will rejoice in the LORD,
I will be joyful in God my Savior.
Habakkuk 3:18

No chain of pearl you wear so adorns you as wisdom.
Thomas Watson

S ally was finishing up her mail route as fast as she could because another winter storm was forecasted for late that afternoon. She hoped to get her mail truck back to the post office and be headed home before the icy snow mix hit. At the very end of the last street of Sally's route lived Angie, an older widowed woman whom Sally had befriended. Sally always made sure she took special care to carry any heavy packages to the door for Angie. Today would be no exception. Pulling into Angie's driveway, Sally put the truck in park and went around to the back to unload the heavy parcel.

She hefted up that box like the pro she was and walked up the steps. She then noticed Angie through the kitchen window and was startled at what she saw: Angie with no hair. Angie saw her and opened the door, her face bright red. "I wasn't expecting you today, Sally. Now you know what I really look like these days."

Sally looked closely at her. "I didn't know you wore a wig. Have you been ill?"

"Yes, I've been going through chemotherapy for my cancer, but we hope that I'm in remission now," she said with a half-smile. "I'll find out next month after more tests."

"Angie, I wish you would have told me," Sally said with concern. "I would have been praying for you. We're friends, right?"

"It happened so fast, it was all I could do to keep up with my doctor appointments, and then I had to have surgery. My daughter flew in for a week during that time. Then I had chemo, and I was so weak and wiped out, I wasn't much in the mood to see anybody. I know it's silly, but aside from the cancer, what I hate most is losing my hair. I feel so . . . vulnerable without it! And I know it makes people uncomfortable to see me bald. I look so different. And then there are all the questions. People mean well, but it wears me out."

"Well, I can't fault you for not wanting to go into all that detail with everyone. But I have a secret to share with you." Sally smiled mischievously as she pulled off her winter hat and watched Angie gape at her. "I haven't had a single hair on my body since I was thirty-five," Sally explained. "It's called Alopecia. I'm completely hairless. So I do understand what you're feeling. It's just that I've had time to get used to it. I had to." Sally said with a lighthearted shrug. "For me, it's permanent."

"Oh, Sally! I'm so embarrassed. Here I am complaining about losing my hair that I know will grow back . . . I'm so sorry."

Sally moved closer to Angie and gave her shoulders a gentle squeeze. "Please don't apologize. I've had years to get used to my new normal, and it doesn't bother me anymore. When I realized my condition wasn't going to change, God helped me accept myself and the way I looked. He helped me gain a better perspective on all the outward stuff by giving me peace and joy on the inside. I have Jesus, and he's all I need. He's all any of us needs."

With tears in their eyes, they hugged each other before Sally went back out to complete her mail route. "See you soon, Angie!" she called as she backed out of Angie's driveway—glad that the storm seemed to be holding off until she could get safely home.

After Sally drove off, Angie smiled to herself and then prayed, *Dear God, I want what Sally has . . . I want peace and joy. I want Jesus . . .*

This story—this perfectly imperfect real-life experience from two women's very different perspectives. Who among us can't relate to the loss Angie felt after battling a serious illness, which had a dramatic effect on her outward appearance? When we endure any kind of trial, there is the accompanying pain, suffering, and loss. And do we ever feel those losses! As recovering perfectionists, losses take their toll on us mentally, physically, emotionally, and even spiritually. We so want to believe we have the power, resources, abilities, and ideas to make it all go away (or all better).

But in real life, perfectionist or not, real people like you and me have to remind ourselves every single day that we are under the care and keeping of our divine heavenly Father. One of the most beautiful aspects of this story is how God, as only God can, orchestrated a beautiful intersection between two women who didn't realize they had a hidden suffering in common.

How wonderfully freeing it must have been for Angie to be truly seen and understood. What joy! How blessed Sally must have felt after she revealed her own similar state of nakedness to her friend Angie. In that divine intersection, both women experienced joy in their own particular ways. Sally, further along in accepting her situation, still needed to embrace the truth that her worth has nothing to do with how she looks. Truly, Sally has learned to say, "I will rejoice in the LORD, I will be joyful in God my Savior." Angie, too, is now learning the same tune.

We all need to make this choice every single day, because our lives will always be cluttered and messy and not quite what we expected. But we can have peace. We can have joy. We can have Jesus, who transforms our perfectly imperfect suffering (inside and out) into something holy (and beautiful to behold).

 ## Take-away Action Thought

When I start to lose my joy because I'm focused on my suffering, I will shut myself away and meditate on this verse: "I will rejoice in the LORD, I will be joyful in God my Savior." This verse will be on my lips and in my heart forevermore.

My Heart's Cry to You, O Lord

Father, when I woke up this morning, there was a short space of time before I remembered what I am facing. I was so happy. So joyfully expectant of starting a new day. Then I felt the sudden stab of pain, the familiar weaknesses, and the losses sweep back over me. Please help me to learn to rejoice in you, to be joyful in you, my Savior, no matter what situation I find myself in. Give me your divine wisdom to accept with good grace this trial, this season of suffering. Please help me to focus on building up my inner self, even though my physical body may be growing weaker. Lord, I am all yours, and I am thankful to be your child. Amen.

Giving Thanks for My Perfectly Imperfect Life

1. Today, I will locate seven Bible verses with the word *joy* in them. I will copy these verses down on note cards and carry them with me wherever I go. In the morning, at noon, and at night, I will read through each verse slowly and meditate on them.

2. This week, I will spend time reflecting on my joy "quotient" and prayerfully ask the Lord to show me how to maintain my joy more consistently. I will consider those "triggers" that seem to discourage, defeat, or depress me. Then I will search out a Bible promise to combat the specific areas in which I'm most likely to struggle.

3. Sometime this week, I will spend time praying for wisdom to navigate through the trials I'm facing. I'll seek the Lord's counsel on how to become more mindful of what is most important in life, and ask him to help me see the opportunities hidden amid the struggles.

 Chapter 25

Perfectly Imperfect—Our Eye on Eternity

But you . . . pursue righteousness, godliness, faith, love, endurance and gentleness. Fight the good fight of the faith. Take hold of the eternal life to which you were called when you made your good confession in the presence of many witnesses.

1 Timothy 6:11–12

The settled happiness and security which we all desire, God withholds from us by the very nature of the world: but joy, pleasure, and merriment, He has scattered broadcast. We are never safe, but we have plenty of fun, and some ecstasy. It is not hard to see why. The security we crave would teach us to rest our hearts in this world and oppose an obstacle to our return to God: a few moments of happy love, a landscape, a symphony, a merry meeting with our friends, a bathe or a football match, have no such tendency. Our Father refreshes us on the journey with some pleasant inns, but will not encourage us to mistake them for home.

C. S. Lewis

O n a recent visit across the state of Michigan to see our oldest daughter and her family, I was looking forward to celebrating three birthdays while there—my daughter and two of our grandsons. As is their custom when one of their three boys turns another year older, my son-in-law retrieves the door-length wooden frame (removed from their former home) and measures their growth. I stood happily watching as my youngest grandson stood on tiptoe, until my daughter told him to stand flat-footed for an accurate measurement! But I totally understood why Jon wanted to be measured taller than he really was. We all want to believe we've grown more than we have in the past year, don't we? I know I do.

Every year around my birthday, I'm a lot like my grandsons. I desire to be more mature and be seen by others as "more grown up." My heart's desire isn't content with minuscule, barely there, strides toward maturity. No, I want to see progress by leaps and bounds away from my sinful, self-centered perfectionist tendencies. I want to be sure that I have been pursuing righteousness, godliness, faith, love, endurance, and gentleness. I want to know that I have fought the good fight of the faith, with my eyes set on eternity. I obviously expect a lot!

Recently, I discovered my friends expect the same from themselves too. As I was sitting among other like-minded, eternity-bound friends, we were discussing this very topic of wanting to see measurable growth in our lives concerning that which matters eternally. Each of us told stories about ourselves and lamented about how frequently we get sidetracked by the mundane happenings of life. Through tears, one friend recalled how all during her two-year fight with cancer, she passionately and persistently shared the love of Jesus with anyone in the waiting areas of the hospital. She felt compelled to spread the same hope she had found in Jesus during her near-death battle with cancer. Now, eight years post-cancer treatments, she admits to not feeling the same urgency she once experienced when death was a viable daily threat. Thoughts of eternity have taken second place to the happenings of daily life.

I, too, recall that same intense desire to share my faith during the months between my father-in-law's esophageal cancer diagnosis and his death. During those brief five months as I sat with him in various waiting rooms and transported him back and forth to the hospital for his daily radiation treatments, I witnessed the miraculous change from a once depressed, anxiety-ridden man to one who was fearless, full of life, and totally at peace. From my perspective, it was as though the veil between this life and the next was paper-thin. I never wanted to lose that eternity focused mind-set I experienced during my father-in-law's final season of life. But sadly, soon after he died, I slowly but surely found myself once again getting caught up in mundane things.

I liken my imperfect, slow walk toward that which matters most in eternity to a fight. It is a daily battle not just to stay alive, but to thrive under the most challenging of circumstances (and the daily mundane ones as well) by firmly taking hold of eternal life and all of its implications to me and others. Our journey to eternity is never perfect and often not very pretty, but it's the journey we all have to make.

Given the tumultuous state of affairs stateside and worldwide, I've been contemplating eternity more and more. I've become far more heavenly minded in recent years, and I recently listened to several series on how we should continue to focus on our hope of Jesus' return. One statement, however, stuck out to me more than any other: "Occupy until Jesus' return." What does that mean? In simple terms, the teacher was exhorting us to be about our Master's work until he comes again and calls us home. Do all the earthly good you can, for as long as you can.

Before he ascended into heaven, Jesus' message to his disciples was clear: Go and tell.

Go into all the world and tell the good news of the gospel. We need to live out Jesus' commands by loving our neighbor (near and far) as well as (or better than) we love ourselves. "Occupy until Jesus returns" means that we also do the next thing we see in front of us, despite any fears or weaknesses. We get up in the morning and ask the Lord for guidance for the day. Then we get moving. Serving. Working. Laboring in love. Ministering one to another. Holding each other up in prayer. Hanging on tight when the need arises. Fighting the good fight of the faith—in perfectly imperfect ways, but fighting on regardless.

We need to remember to view our perfectly imperfect progress through the lens of God's grace and mercy, because we will falter, we will fail, and we will want to give up. But we won't because we, though perfectly imperfect, understand that we are called to fight the good fight of the faith, and we want to take hold of the eternal life to which we are called. Remember, God doesn't want us to view this world as our permanent home. Day by day, we need to choose to pursue righteousness, godliness, faith, love, endurance, and gentleness, all the while keeping the hope of eternity burning brightly in our hearts.

 Take-away Action Thought

When I become sidetracked by the mundane happenings of daily life and lose my eternal focus, I will purposefully follow the pray/think/act plan to reorder my thinking and my priorities.

My Heart's Cry to You, O Lord

Father, I'm so slow to learn, and sometimes I feel as though I'm not growing at all. I long to see leaps and bounds of change in my life, but I rarely do. I see myself stepping forward two steps and then falling back three. My perfectionist tendencies serve only to frustrate me, and then I want to give up. Help me to accept that this walk of faith is sometimes a battle. Help me to remember that this is not my home, that heaven is my home. I'm just passing through this world. Remind me to be eternally minded by focusing on that which matters most: people's souls. I need your wisdom, grace, and strength to fight the good fight of the faith. I rely on your supernatural empowerment every moment of every day. Amen.

Giving Thanks for My Perfectly Imperfect Life

1. "Pursue righteousness, godliness, faith, love, endurance and gentleness." This week, I will reflect on my growth toward maturity by prayerfully considering how consistent I am in pursuing these character qualities.

2. "Fight the good fight of the faith." I will spend time in prayer, asking the Lord to help me fully accept and understand that the Christian walk is a daily battle. I will memorize Ephesians 6:14–17, which describes the full armor of God and how it readies me for life's battles.

3. "Take hold of the eternal life to which you were called when you made your good confession in the presence of many witnesses." I will reflect on my confession of faith, my public act of obedience in baptism, and how much it impacts others when I speak about my faith. This week, I will spend time in prayer, asking the Lord to help me keep my mind focused on that which matters for eternity.

Sources for Quotations

1. Elisabeth Elliot, *Keep a Quiet Heart* (Grand Rapids: Baker, 2004).

2. Oswald Chambers, *My Utmost for His Highest* (Grand Rapids: Discovery House, 1992), December 31 entry.

3. Tim Lane and Paul Tripp, *Relationships: A Mess Worth Making* (Greensboro: New Growth Press, 2006), 110–11.

4. Elisabeth Elliot, *The Path of Loneliness: Finding Your Way through the Wilderness to God* (repr., Grand Rapids: Revell, 2007).

5. Jerry Bridges, *Trusting God* (Colorado Springs: NavPress, 1988), 112.

6. Max Lucado, *Anxious for Nothing: Finding Calm in a Chaotic World* (Nashville: Thomas Nelson, 2017), 99.

7. Nancy Leigh DeMoss, *Choosing Forgiveness: Your Journey to Freedom* (Chicago: Moody, 2008), 45–46.

8. Bridges, *Trusting God*, 18.

9. Chambers, *My Utmost for His Highest*, October 21 entry.

10. Nancy Leigh DeMoss, *Choosing Gratitude: Your Journey to Joy* (Chicago: Moody, 2009), 63.

11. Bridges, *Trusting God*, 45.

12. Chambers, *My Utmost for His Highest*, October 1 entry.

13. Richard Burr, *Praying Your Prodigal Home: Unleashing God's Power to Set Your Loved Ones Free* (repr., Chicago: WingSpread / Moody, 2008), 26.

14. Elisabeth Elliot, *Suffering Is Never for Nothing* (repr., Nashville: B&H, 2019), ch. 3.

15. Elyse Fitzpatrick, *Found in Him: The Joy of the Incarnation and Our Union with Christ* (Wheaton: Crossway, 2013), 203.

16. Chambers, *My Utmost for His Highest*, January 31 entry.

17. Bridges, *Trusting God*, 52.

18. Linda Dillow, *Calm My Anxious Heart* (Carol Stream, IL: NavPress, 2007), 15.

19. Arthur G. Bennett, ed., *The Valley of Vision: A Collection of Puritan Prayers and Devotions* (Carlisle, PA: Banner of Truth Trust, 2007), 48–49.

20. Tim Keller, *The Freedom of Self-Forgetfulness: The Path to True Christian Joy* (Leyland, UK: 10Publishing, 2012).

21. DeMoss, *Choosing Forgiveness*, 156.

22. DeMoss, *Choosing Forgiveness*, 114.

23. Fitzpatrick, *Found in Him*, 110.

24. Thomas Watson, "Of Wisdom and Innocency," *A Body of Practical Divinity; Consisting of Above One Hundred and Seventy-Six Sermons on the Shorter Catechism* (n.p.: Arkose Press, 2015), 593.

25. C. S. Lewis, *The Problem of Pain* (New York: Macmillan, 1962), 115.